ENCUENTROS CULTURALES CROSS-

PC411

A12464

D0978735

DATE DUE

AP 17 '95			
DE 22 '95			
SE 15 '97			
FE 17 '98			
MR 18 '99			

Encuentros culturales

Cross-cultural mini-dramas

Barbara Snyder

H. Ned Seelye
Consulting Editor

National Textbook Company
a division of *NTC Publishing Group* • Lincolnwood, Illinois USA

Acknowledgment

«Yo te amo sol»

E. Herman Hespelt, *An Anthology of Spanish American Literature*, 1946. Reprinted by permission of Prentice-Hall, Inc., Englewood Cliffs, New Jersey.

1994 Printing

Published by National Textbook Company, a division of NTC Publishing Group.
© 1990, 1984, 1975 by NTC Publishing Group, 4255 West Touhy Avenue.
Lincolnwood (Chicago), Illinois 60646-1975 U.S.A.
Manufactured in the United States of America.
Library of Congress Catalog Card Number: 75-21045

3 4 5 6 7 8 9 0 ML 9 8 7 6 5 4 3

How To Use This Book

The mini-dramas in this book involve American teenagers and Spanish-speaking teenagers and their families. The American is an exchange student living with a family in a Spanish-speaking country. (In a few mini-dramas, a Spanish-speaking teenager is living with an American family).

Living in another country can be full of surprises and can also create unexpected problems. That is what this book is about: various areas of life that are different in different countries. Each mini-drama involves a difference, and after reading or listening to the mini-drama, you are asked to decide the reason for this difference. A question is posed, and after each question there are four possible solutions. Although there may be some truth in more than one answer, you are asked to decide on the best possible answer to the question. After you have decided what the solution is, turn to the page indicated and read the follow-up for that answer. It will explain why you are right and give further information, or it will explain why you have not chosen the best answer. Quite often it will give you a clue so that you can go back and choose the correct answer.

When you travel to a Spanish-speaking country, knowing about some of these differences will help you better understand your Spanish-speaking friends. If a new mini-drama occurs in your life, you can think up several possible explanations for the situation and have an interesting time discovering the real answer.

Contents

Introduction

In a world that is becoming increasingly interconnected by jet travel and modern telecommunications, *Encuentros culturales* fills a real and important need. With increasing frequency, men and women from differing cultures are coming in contact and learning the often difficult lesson of how to communicate with one another. These meetings with people from other countries and cultures can be full of surprises and cause unforeseen problems. This book treats such cultural dilemmas directly. Each mini-drama in this collection demonstrates the fact that attitudes, values, beliefs, expectations, roles, and life-styles tend to be viewed in varying ways in various cultures.

After each of the mini-dramas in this book, students are asked a question and offered four possible solutions. They are then instructed to check their answers. If they select an incorrect answer the first time, clues and further information are provided to help them find the right solution.

These mini-dramas serve equally well as a mini-course, as supplementary material, or as a self-study text. Though units are ordered according to language difficulty, they are all self-contained. Thus, concepts discussed in them may be covered in the order in which they appear in the basal text used in class. In so far as pacing is concerned, the 53 mini-dramas in *Encuentros culturales* may be used at a rate of about one a week during a single year, or two a month over two years.

In preparing this cultural material, the author was guided by three basic objectives: 1) Students should appreciate that cultural differences, not just language differences, exist between and among countries; 2) Students who travel to a Spanish-speaking among countries; 2) Students who travel to a Spanish-speaking country should experience fewer difficulties arising from cultural conflict; 3) If cultural conflict does occur, a student should be able to solve it intelligently because of his or her experience with hypothesis testing. In this way, the trauma of "culture shock" will be reduced significantly.

In connection with these cultural mini-dramas, the teacher may wish to lead students in a discussion that highlights the relativity of cultural modes. A discussion of this kind could emphasize the point that there is no *one* right way of acting or thinking—that a variety of legitimate responses may exist. As further work, students may wish to continue the dialogue at the point at which the North American begins to understand. They may also create a new mini-drama showing the American student responding appropriately to a situation.

The author hopes that *Encuentros culturales* will help students deepen their knowledge of foreign cultures and languages and that it will encourage increased understanding of cultural diversity. Other National Textbook Company publications also contribute to these objectives. *Teaching Culture: Strategies for Intercultural Communication* by H. Ned Seelye describes the acquisition of cultural skills and discusses the process by which we acquire cultural characteristics. This is the first book ever devoted completely to the methodology of conveying cultural concepts in communications classes. The second book in this series is Raymond Gorden's *Living in Latin America: A Case Study in Cross-Cultural Communication*, which treats the nature of communication as a combination of fluency in both the language and the non-verbal cultural patterns that accompany it. The third volume, *The Newspaper: Spanish Mini-Culture Unit* by H. Ned Seelye and J. Laurence Day provides the classroom teacher with practical handouts to help students experience cultural insights firsthand through Hispanic newspapers.

1. ¡Jesús!

San Salvador, El Salvador

Mark: Hola, Beto.
Beto: Hola, Mark. ¿Cómo estás?
Mark: Estoy bien, gracias. ¿Y tú?
Beto: Muy bien. Mark, ¡éste es mi buen amigo, Jesús!
Jesús, Mark es de los Estados Unidos.
Mark: Mucho gusto.
Amigo: El gusto es mío.

(Más tarde)

Beto: Lo siento, pero tengo que irme.
¡Hasta luego, Mark! ¡Adiós, Jesús!
Mark: Adiós, hasta luego.

Why does Beto keep swearing?

A. Beto really is not swearing because saying Jesús is not considered swearing in San Salvador. (Turn to page 75, A)
B. Beto really is not swearing because his friend's name is Jesús. (Turn to page 71, B)
C. Beto really is not swearing because Mark is sneezing and this is what one says for a sneeze. (Turn to page 105, C)
D. Beto really is not swearing because his friend is studying to be a priest and this is the proper form of address. (Turn to page 59, D)

2. María

Monterrey, México

Ann: ¿Qué haces, Juanita?
Juanita: Escribo una carta a mi amigo José.
Ann: Pues, por favor. No quiero llegar tarde al cine.
Juanita: Entonces, ¿quieres ayudarme? Aquí está la dirección. Favor de escribírmela en el sobre.°

> José María Sánchez Bonilla
> Avenida Zapata 102
> México, D. F.

Ann: O. K. (La escribe.) Terminada. Aquí está. Vámonos.

> José Mario Sánchez Bonilla
> Avenida Zapata 102
> México, D. F.

Juanita: ¡Ay! Ann, no es correcto el nombre. Es José María en vez de José Mario.
Ann: José es hombre, ¿verdad?
Juanita: Sí, claro.
Ann: No entiendo. ¿Tiene el nombre María?

Why is Ann confused about José's name?

A. Ann does not realize that it is customary to put the mother's first name on the letter also. (Turn to page 78, A)
B. Juanita has made a mistake and does not want to admit it. (Turn to page 100, B)
C. Although María is the most common girl's name, Ann does not realize that it is also a common second name for boys in many p⌐..ts of Latin America, and that the name José María is acceptable for boys. (Turn to page 72, C)
D. In Latin America, it is customary to have several «first» names. The boys usually have their mother's name as one of them. (Turn to page 105, D)

---

sobre envelope

2

3. ¿Luis?

Una fuente de sodas, Mayagüez, Puerto Rico

Belita: Nancy, éste es mi buen amigo, Luis Pérez Villarreal.
Nancy: Mucho gusto en conocerte, Luis.
Luis: El gusto es mío, Nancy.

(Más tarde)

Nancy: ¿Conoces a ese chico tan guapo, Luis Villarreal?
Mela: No, creo que no lo conozco. ¿Es de aquí?
Nancy: Sí, creo. Es buen amigo de Belita.
Mela: ¿De Belita? Belita es mi amiga. ¿Cómo se llama el chico?
Nancy: Luis Villarreal.
Mela: Conozco a varios chicos que se llaman Luis. Es un nombre corriente° por acá. Y también conozco a la familia Villarreal. Pero, ¿quién es ese Luis Villarreal?

Why doesn't Mela know who Luis is?

A. Nancy has mistaken his name. (Turn to p. 66, A)
B. It is not polite for Latin American girls to admit that they know someone else's boyfriend. Although Mela knows who Luis is, she will not admit it. (Turn to p. 63, B)
C. Girls do not go to the same school as boys do; therefore the girls really do not get to know many boys. (Turn to p. 93, C)
D. Girls cannot admit that they know a boy unless they have met him formally. (Turn to p. 64, D)

---

corriente common

4. Adiós

Una calle, San Miguel de Allende, México

Patty:	Mira, ¿no es ésa la Sra. Rodríguez?
Abuela:	Sí, Patty. Aprendes muy rápidamente quienes son todos.
Patty:	Sí. Nacho dice que es tu amiga.
Abuela:	No, la conozco, pero no muy bien. Aquí viene.
Sra. Rodríguez:	Adiós.
Abuela:	Adiós.
Patty:	¿Adiós?

(Más tarde)

Patty:	Creo que estoy aprendiendo muy rápidamente el español aquí en México.
Amalia:	Sí, es verdad. Hablas mucho mejor.
Patty:	Aquí viene Lola Ramírez. Adiós, Lola.
Lola:	¿Adiós? Acabo de llegar.° Hola, Patty. Es difícil aprender otra lengua, ¿no?
Patty:	¿Otro error? ¡Oh, no!

Why did Patty make another mistake?

A. Although Amalia is trying to make her feel better, Patty really is not learning Spanish very well. (Turn to p. 70, A)

B. *Adiós* is the slang way to say hello. (Turn to p. 107, B)

C. Older people say *adiós* because they may never see each other again. Younger people say something like *hasta luego*. (Turn to p. 66, C)

D. *Adiós* is the greeting used when passing each other in the street. (Turn to p. 71, D)

---

acabo de llegar I have just arrived

5. Una tortilla, por favor

Toman el desayuno, un restaurante, Madrid, España

Paco: Tengo hambre. Quiero jugo de naranja, una tortilla de queso y café.
Julie: ¿No vas a comer más que una tortilla?
Paco: No, es suficiente.
Julie: Para mí, huevos fritos, pan tostado y un vaso de leche, por favor.

(Llega el desayuno.)

Julie: Paco, ¿quieres huevos?
Paco: Sí, me gustan.
Julie: ¿Y la tortilla? ¿No la quieres entonces?
Paco: Por supuesto. ¿Por qué preguntas eso?

What has Julie confused?

A. Julie still does not understand Spanish very well and she thought Paco ordered a cheese sandwich. (Turn to p. 84, A)
B. Julie wishes she had ordered tortillas and is hinting for Paco to give her some. (Turn to p. 106, B)
C. Paco needs to go on a diet and Julie cannot understand why he is eating so much. (Turn to p. 92, C)
D. Julie does not realize that tortilla has a different meaning in Spain than in Mexico. (Turn to p. 81, D)

6. Está deliciosa

Un restaurante, Madrid, España

Camarero:	Buenas noches. ¿Qué desean tomar?
Jaime:	Para mí, gazpacho, arroz con pollo, una ensalada de lechuga° y café.
Sally:	¿Qué es gazpacho?
Jaime:	Es una sopa española muy sabrosa, una sopa de tomate con legumbres...
Sally:	Entonces, yo también la quiero. Y para mí, paella valenciana, ensalada y una Coca-Cola.
Camarero:	Bien, gracias.

(Más tarde)

Camarero:	Aquí está el gazpacho y pongo aquí en la mesa la cebolla,° los pepinos°...
Jaime:	¡Esta sopa está deliciosa!
Sally:	Ay, Jaime, lo siento pero la sopa está fría.
Jaime:	Claro, está bien fría.
Sally:	No está caliente, Jaime. ¿Cómo está la tuya?
Jaime:	Excelente. ¿No te gusta?
Sally:	Es que está fría. Hazme el favor de llamar al camarero.
Jaime:	Si quieres, pero el gazpacho está muy sabroso. Pero la sopa de cebolla está buena también y está caliente.

Why doesn't Sally like the *gazpacho*?

A. Sally prefers Mexican soup. (Turn to p. 82, A)
B. It needs to be warmed up. (Turn to p. 94, B)
C. *Gazpacho* is not really a tomato soup. (Turn to p. 76, C)
D. Jaime forgot to tell her that *gazpacho* is served chilled. (Turn to p. 67, D)

---

lechuga lettuce   **cebolla** onion   **pepinos** cucumbers

6

7. El vino

Un restaurante, Viña del Mar, Chile

Camarero:	¿Qué desean Uds.?
Papá:	Para mí, la paella.
Mamá:	Para mí también.
Camarero:	¿Y el vino?
Papá:	El vino blanco.
Pilar:	Papá, ¿puedo comer una hamburguesa?
Papá:	Claro que sí.
Pilar:	Entonces, quiero una hamburguesa con queso y papas fritas.
Jill:	Yo también.

(Llega el almuerzo.)

Pilar:	Esta hamburguesa está deliciosa. Y también el vino.
Jill:	Pilar, ¿tomas vino?
Pilar:	Claro. Lo siento, Jill. No tienes vino. Papá, pásame el vino, por favor.
Papá:	Aquí está.
Jill:	No, no. Yo no quiero vino.
Pilar:	Yo sí. Una copa° más para mí.
Jill:	Pilar, tú solamente tienes 16 años, ¿verdad?
Pilar:	Sí, ¿por qué?
Jill:	Es que... ¿Tu papá permite...? El vino...
Pilar:	¿Quieres vino? Tómalo. Es un vino muy bueno. Es de Chile.

Why is Pilar permitted to drink wine?

A. Young people are permitted to drink Chilean wine. (Turn to p. 99, A)
B. Her father believes that young people should learn to drink alcoholic beverages under the supervision of their parents. (Turn to p. 85, B)
C. Young people in Chile only have to be 15 to drink wine. (Turn to p. 96, C)
D. Wine is customarily served with meals and there are no laws against it. (Turn to p. 80, D)

---

copa wineglass

7

8. Nuevos amigos

San Juan, Puerto Rico

Eduardo:	Mamá, David y yo salimos. Vámonos, David. Aquí viene Julián, mi hermano mayor. Tú ya no lo conoces. Julián, éste es David García de Nueva York. Es sobrino de los Fernández. David, mi hermano, Julián Marín Baldillo.
David:	Mucho gusto.
Julián:	El gusto es mío. Y David y Eduardo, quiero presentarles a mi compadre Gregorio Vega.
Gregorio:	Mucho gusto.
Julián:	Gregorio piensa ir a Pennsylvania el mes que viene,° ¿eh, compadre?
Gregorio:	Sí, David, así es que quiero invitarte a cenar con mi familia esta noche.
David:	Muchas gracias. Me gustaría mucho.
Gregorio:	Excelente. Tú vas también, ¿verdad, compadre?
Julián:	Con mucho gusto. Tu mamá siempre sirve una comida muy sabrosa.
Eduardo:	Claro, con razón. ¿No es ella comadre del mejor cocinero de San Juan, el del Restaurante... Zaragozana?
Gregorio:	(Riendo) Es cierto. Y tú también tienes invitación para cenar con nosotros esta noche.
Eduardo:	Para disfrutar de° la mejor comida puertorriqueña que hay, acepto con muchas gracias.
Gregorio:	Entonces, todos nos veremos esta noche, a las ocho.
Eduardo:	Está bien.
Julián:	De acuerdo. Ven, compadre. Vamos a llegar tarde.
David:	Hasta luego.

Why are they calling each other _compadre_?

A. It is used only for very special or very close friends. (Turn to p. 59, A)
B. It is another word for cousin. (Turn to p. 68, B)
C. It is a word like _hombre_ or _chico_ that can be applied to everyone. (Turn to p. 80, C)
D. It is a slang term something like «Tiger» in English. (Turn to p. 92, D)

---

el mes que viene next month   **disfrutar de** to enjoy

8

9. ¿Fútbol?

Sábado por la tarde, Santiago, Chile

Carlos: ¿Quieres ir conmigo a ver un partido de fútbol?
Tom: Claro que sí. Yo juego al fútbol en los Estados Unidos y por eso me gusta mucho.
Carlos: Bien, entonces mañana podemos jugar al fútbol con mis amigos. Siempre juegan los domingos.
Tom: Gracias. Deseo mucho jugar.

(Al día siguiente, el domingo, el campo de fútbol)

Tom: ¡Ay de mí! ¿Qué es esto? ¡Ay, no! Lo siento mucho, Carlos, pero no puedo jugar al fútbol con ustedes. No sé jugar así.
Carlos: Sí, puedes. No somos expertos.
Tom: No, no entiendes. Es que no juego a ese deporte.
Carlos: Ay, hombre. Sí puedes hacerlo.

Why has Tom changed his mind about playing football?

A. Tom had just eaten a big breakfast and he decided that he had better not. (Turn to p. 94, A)
B. Tom had just been bragging the day before and really does not want them to know he does not play. (Turn to p. 105, B)
C. Tom had not realized that Carlos and his friends were such experts. (Turn to p. 71, C)
D. Tom had not realized that Carlos plays a different kind of football than is played in the U. S. (Turn to p. 84, D)

9

10. El cumpleaños

La Ciudad de Guatemala, Guatemala

Cristóbal: El miércoles que viene es tu cumpleaños, ¿verdad?
Chuck: Sí, el ocho de julio. ¿Cómo lo sabes?
Cristóbal: Mamá lo sabe. Las mujeres siempre saben de estas cosas. Además, es buena oportunidad para dar una fiesta. Tú sabes que las mujeres están locas por las fiestas, ¿no?
Chuck: ¡Qué amable es ella! Bueno, ¿cuándo es tu cumpleaños?
Cristóbal: Pues, es el día diez de este mes.
Chuck: Es el viernes que viene. ¿Por qué no lo celebramos juntos?
Cristóbal: Casi nunca lo celebro ese día. Acostumbro a celebrarlo el 24 de este mes que es mi santo.
Chuck: ¿No celebras tu cumpleaños? Pues, este año puedes celebrarlo conmigo.
Cristóbal: Sí, lo celebro, pero mi santo es en quince días. Y además, podemos dar otra fiesta entonces.

Why doesn't Cristóbal want to celebrate his own birthday?

A. Guatemalans can choose their own day to celebrate. (Turn to p. 91, A)
B. Latin Americans often celebrate their name day rather than their birthday, and Cristóbal follows this custom. (Turn to p. 84, B)
C. The women select a day somewhere near a person's birthday that is a good day on which to have a party, and the family celebrates the birthday then. (Turn to p. 108, C)
D. Cristóbal prefers to celebrate with his godfather on his birthday. (Turn to p. 77, D)

11. Día de fiesta

Asunción, Paraguay

Bárbara: El lunes voy a ir de compras. ¿Quieres ir también?
Pam: Sí, quiero comprar algo de ñandutí° para el cumpleaños de mi mamá.
Bárbara: Muy bien. Es un regalo muy bueno.
Pam: ¿Qué vamos a hacer el cuatro de julio?
Bárbara: No sé. Nada de particular. ¿Qué día es?
Pam: El jueves que viene.
Bárbara: Bueno, tengo un examen de filosofía el viernes. Supongo que tenga que estudiar esa noche.
Pam: ¡Qué lástima! ¡Tener que estudiar el cuatro de julio!
Bárbara: ¿Por qué?
Pam: ¡Es un día de fiesta!
Bárbara: Ah, ¿es tu santo? Entonces sí, vamos a hacer algo especial. Podemos celebrarlo con una fiesta.
Pam: No, no es mi santo. Es el cuatro de julio.
Bárbara: ¿Qué es el cuatro de julio?

Why doesn't Bárbara seem to know about the 4th of July?

A. It is wintertime in Paraguay so the 4th of July comes on January 4th. (Turn to p. 88, A)
B. They do not have a 4th of July in Paraguay. (Turn to p. 86, B)
C. In Paraguay, they celebrate the 14th of May. (Turn to p. 59, C)
D. Because of the government, only religious holidays are celebrated in Paraguay. (Turn to p. 96, D)

ñandutí handmade lace

12. Muy macho

En casa de Pedro y Teresa, Durango, México

Felipe: Vámonos, Pedro. Ya llegan Carlos y Juan.
Pedro: Sí, estoy listo. Ahorita vengo. Hasta luego, niñas.
Teresa: Hasta luego. Que lo pasen bien.

(Un poco después)

Teresa: Ay, ¡qué guapo es Felipe! ¿Verdad?
Cheryl: Felipe puede ser guapo pero no me parece muy macho.
Teresa: ¡Cheryl! No digas eso. Es amigo de Pedro y es muy macho. ¿Por qué dices que no es macho?
Cheryl: Pues es verdad. Sí es amigo de Pedro pero, ¡siempre lo *abraza*!°
Teresa: Sí, claro se abrazan. Son buenos amigos.
Cheryl: Pero, Teresa, ¡Felipe deja el brazo sobre los hombros de Pedro!
Teresa: Son amigos. No entiendo por qué te preocupas° tanto. Te digo que Felipe es muy macho.

What is bothering Cheryl?

A. Felipe is teasing her by going out with Pedro and not paying any attention to her. (Turn to p. 80, A)
B. Cheryl is for women's lib and does not like boys who are *macho*. (Turn to p. 72, B)
C. Cheryl does not think Felipe should act quite so «friendly» with Pedro. (Turn to p. 73, C)
D. Pedro has been sick but he is fine now and Felipe keeps treating him like an invalid. (Turn to p. 74, D)

---

abraza hugs, embraces   **te preocupas** you worry

12

13. ¡Qué salerosas!

*Dos chicas negras dan un paseo°   por Santo Domingo,
la República Dominicana.*

Sandra: Hace calor aquí, ¿verdad?
Doris: Sí, pero la brisa del mar lo hace menos malo.
Sandra: Me gusta Santo Domingo. No quiero salir mañana.
Joven: ¡Señoritas norteamericanas! ¡Qué salerosas!°
Sandra: ¿Quién es? ¿Tú lo conoces?
Doris: No, no lo conozco.
Sandra: Ni yo tampoco.
Joven: ¡Qué bonita eres, negrita! Y tú, también, piel° canela.°
Doris: ¡Qué rudo! ¡No nos insulte! Váyase. Vente, Sandra.
Sandra: Sí, este hombre es horrible. Estoy muy enojada. Ahora sí quiero salir.
Joven: ¿Qué pasa? ¿Qué digo que es malo? Esperen, señoritas.

Why are the girls so angry?

A. The girls consider the term *negrita* an insult. (Turn to p. 74, A)
B. The man is a thief and is trying to rob them. (Turn to p. 80, B)
C. Men do not talk to «nice» girls unless they know them. (Turn to p. 86, C)
D. The girls think that Americans should be respected. (Turn to p. 76, D)

---

dan un paseo taking a walk
salerosas charming

piel skin
canela cinnamon

14. El paseo

En casa de Alicia Meléndez, Taxco, México

Carol: Alicia, Miguel quiere ir conmigo al paseo.
Alicia: ¡Qué bueno, chica!
Carol: ¿Bueno? ¿Ir de paseo? De veras, no quiero ir. Yo quiero ir al cine. Hay una buena película esta semana.
Alicia: ¡Ay, chica! Se puede ir al cine otro día. Todos vamos al paseo. ¡Es muy divertido!
Carol: ¿Por qué no podemos ir de paseo otro día?
Alicia: Sólo hay paseo el domingo. Y dan un concierto también.
Carol: Pues, ¿por qué no vamos al concierto?
Alicia: Sí, vamos al concierto. Está en el jardín, el zócalo.°
Carol: Si vamos al concierto, ¿cómo podemos pasear?
Alicia: ¡Ay de mí! Si no vamos al paseo, no oímos el concierto. Carol, te va a gustar mucho el paseo. De veras.

Why are Carol and Alicia failing to communicate about this?

A. *Paseo* is a concert and Carol does not understand the meaning of the word. (Turn to p. 64, A)
B. The *paseo* is not just taking a walk but is a social event, like a picnic, a dance, etc. Carol does not realize this. (Turn to p. 58, B)
C. Mexican girls like going for walks more than American girls and that is what Alicia would most like to do. Carol does not agree. (Turn to p. 84, C)
D. Carol really does not like Miguel. She is trying to get out of going anywhere with him without hurting Alicia's feelings. (Turn to p. 94, D)

---

zócalo main square, plaza

15. Ocho días

El paseo, Taxco, México

Carol: ¡Qué divertido es el paseo esta semana!
Miguel: ¡Y qué buena la banda!
Alicia: Ojalá que no termine muy pronto.
Tomás: Sí, nos divertimos mucho. Carol y Miguel, ¿vamos otra vez la semana que viene?
Miguel: Cómo no. Nos gustaría mucho ir con ustedes.
Carol: Muchísimo.
Alicia: Entonces, nos vemos en ocho días. Hasta luego.
Miguel: Hasta la vista.
Tomás: Adiós, amigos. (Se van.)
Carol: ¿No vamos el domingo que viene?
Miguel: Sí, claro. Siempre dan los conciertos los domingos y Tomás y Alicia nos invitaron.
Carol: Entonces, ¿vamos otra vez el lunes?
Miguel: ¿El lunes? No hay paseo el lunes. ¿Por qué preguntas eso?

Why does Carol seem to be confused about when they are going to the next *paseo?*

A. Carol does not understand why Tomás said they would see each other in eight days instead of a week. (Turn to p. 57, A)
B. Carol thought that this *paseo* was for a special fiesta. (Turn to p. 67, B)
C. Carol thinks the concert is Sunday, so the *paseo* must be some other night. (Turn to p. 78, C)
D. Carol thinks there is a *paseo* every night. (Turn to p. 99, D)

16. Una fiesta

Esperan a Isabel, en casa, Cali, Colombia.

Scott: Isabel todavía no está lista. Vamos a llegar muy tarde. Empieza la fiesta a las nueve y ya son las nueve y media.

Ramón: No te preocupes, Scott. Todavía tenemos mucho tiempo. Carlota, ¿por qué no tocas un disco mientras esperamos?

Carlota: Muy buena idea. Isabel tiene un nuevo álbum por Julio Iglesias. ¿Quieres escucharlo?

Ramón: Fantástico. ¿No canta esa canción que ahora está popular en los Estados Unidos? Te va a gustar este álbum, Scott.

Scott: ¿Todo un álbum? Vamos a perder la mitad de la fiesta.

Ramón: No, hombre. Vas a llegar a tiempo para bailar mucho con Isabel.

Scott: No es eso. ¿Qué pensará Roberto? Lo debemos llamar.

Ramón: ¿Por qué? El sabe que vamos. ¿No te gusta la música?

Carlota: Quizá Isabel lleve el álbum a la fiesta.

Scott: Si es que vamos.

Why isn't Ramón worried about being late?

A. Like some men, Ramón would rather not go to the party. He would rather talk to Carlota quietly as long as possible. (Turn to p. 93, A)

B. Ramón does not want to make Scott feel bad because his date is late. Latin Americans are very polite. (Turn to p. 79, B)

C. They are not really late yet by Latin American standards. (Turn to p. 82, C)

D. Ramón does not like Roberto and one way to insult him very subtly is to arrive late at his party. (Turn to p. 86, D)

17. ¡Ay de mí!

Un baile, la Ciudad de Panamá, Panamá

Sue: ¡Mira qué hora es! Casi las dos de la mañana. Debemos salir pronto.

Eliseo: ¿Tan pronto? El baile todavía está animado.

Sue: Pero es muy tarde.

Eliseo: ¿No te gusta la fiesta?

Sue: Claro. Me divierto muchísimo, pero...

Eliseo: Pues, si quieres, dentro de poco salimos.

(Más tarde)

Sue: Dolores, ya son casi las tres. Es hora de salir. ¿Qué dirá tu mamá? ¿Puedes pedir que Eliseo nos lleve a casa?

Dolores: ¿Ahora? Pues, la fiesta está muy alegre. ¿No te gusta?

Sue: Pero, ¿a qué hora termina?

Dolores: ¿Quién sabe? Quizá a las cinco.

Sue: ¡A las cinco! ¿Y vas a quedarte?

Dolores: No sé, pero el baile va muy bien y... Aquí vienen Eliseo y Tomás.

Eliseo: Vamos, muchacha...

Sue: ¡Al fin! ¡Qué bien!

Eliseo: Esta música es fantástica. Vamos a bailar.

Sue: ¡Ay de mí!

Why are Eliseo and Dolores staying so late at the dance?

A. Occasionally the young Latin Americans are given special permission to stay out very late. (Turn to p. 95, A)

B. For a Latin American dance, it is not late. The dances usually last all night. (Turn to p. 99, B)

C. No one wants to be the first to leave. (Turn to p.106, C)

D. Latin Americans do not have very many dances, so when they do, they make it last as long as possible. (Turn to p. 58, D)

17

18. ¿Otro baile?

Un baile, Valparaíso, Chile

Peggy: ¡Qué alegre es este baile!
Mateo: Tienes razón. Estoy cansado después de bailar media hora de rock.
Peggy: Sí, tengo calor.
Mateo: Yo también y, además, tengo sed. Vamos a tomar unos refrescos.
Peggy: Buena idea.
Mateo: Espérate. ¡Escucha la música! Vamos a bailar éste.
Peggy: ¿Qué baile es éste? No lo reconozco.
Mateo: ¡La cueca! Vámonos.
Peggy: No es rock. Es para los viejos, ¿verdad? ¿Por qué quieres bailar éste?
Mateo: Es la cueca. Yo te enseño. Es muy divertido.
Peggy: Ay, Mateo, no tengo ganas de° bailar ahora.
Mateo: Tienes que bailar solamente este baile. Entonces tomamos refrescos, te prometo. Date prisa,° Peggy.

Why is Mateo insisting on this particular dance?

A. It is a popular folk dance in Chile. (Turn to p. 77, A)
B. Mateo wants to keep on dancing with Peggy. (Turn to p. 103, B)
C. Mateo wants to impress his parents who will be sure to be dancing this one also. (Turn to p. 62, C)
D. A Latin American male should not admit that he is tired. It is a sign of weakness; therefore Paco wants to dance one more. (Turn to p. 82, D)

---

no tengo ganas de I don't feel like   **date prisa** hurry up

18

19. ¿Puedo ayudar?

La casa de los Castro, Lima, Perú

Janie: ¿Puedo ayudar a lavar los platos?
Mamá: No, Janie. ¿Por qué preguntas eso? Lupe los lava.
Janie: Pues, quiero ayudar a Lupe puesto que° ella me hizo la cama esta mañana.
Mamá: Por supuesto que te hizo la cama. Por eso está aquí.
Janie: ¿No hay nada en que puedo ayudar? Les agradezco mucho la hospitalidad.
Mamá: Me alegro de que estés contenta aquí en nuestra casa. Momentito. ¡Lupe! Lupe, trae los pasteles por favor.
Janie: ¿Qué puedo hacer yo?
Mamá: ¿Por qué no van ustedes al cine esta tarde?

Why can't Janie help?

A. The mother is a perfectionist as are many Latin American housewives. Janie cannot be expected to do housework the Latin American way, so Mamá does not want her to help. (Turn to p. 102, A)
B. Guests are never expected to help and Janie is considered a guest. It would be very impolite for them to ask her to help. (Turn to p. 61, B)
C. Latin Americans think all North Americans are rich and the mother does not want to offend Janie by making her work. They are giving her special treatment because she is a North American. (Turn to p. 87, C)
D. Lupe is the maid and it is her job to do the work. Janie and the other family members are not expected to do such jobs. (Turn to p. 65, D)

---

puesto que since

19

20. La película

Durante el descanso entre clases, la Ciudad de México

Víctor: ¿Quieres ir conmigo al cine esta noche?
Jim: ¿Qué película hay? Iba a estudiar esta noche.
Víctor: *Los Olvidados,* un clásico por Luis Buñuel.
Jim: Lo siento, pero quiero ver *El violinista sobre el tejado* ° y le prometí a Carmen que la llevaría mañana.
Víctor: Está bien, hombre. Podemos ver las dos. Vamos hoy tan pronto como terminen las clases y mañana yo llevo a Catalina.
Jim: No, creo que no tengo bastante dinero para hoy y también para mañana.
Víctor: Pues, cuesta muy poco. La película de hoy es solamente setenta* pesos y la de mañana, noventa. ¿No tienes ciento cincuenta pesos? Yo te los presto ° hasta que llegue el dinero de tu papá.
Jim: Gracias, pero no es necesario. Yo voy contigo hoy y mañana llevaremos a las chicas.
Víctor: Bien. Nos vemos después.

Why didn't Jim want to go the movies with Victor at first?

A. Jim was not really interested in seeing a movie by Luis Buñuel. (Turn to p. 90, A)
B. Jim did not think he had enough money. (Turn to p. 57, B)
C. Jim really wanted to study. (Turn to p. 104, C)
D. Carmen cannot go out two nights in a row. (Turn to p. 60, D)

---

*At the beginning of 1984, 1 peso was worth .7 of a U.S. cent.

---

tejado roof   **presto** I will lend

21. Está cerrada

El centro, Madrid, España

Marisol: Ya son las dos. Es hora de comer. Vámonos, Becky.
Becky: Muy bien, pero primero quiero comprar una cosa más. Necesito papel.
Marisol: Pues, no lo puedes comprar ahora. Ya son las dos.
Becky: Sí, pero no tarda. Solamente un momentito.
Marisol: Pero la tienda está cerrada.
Becky: ¿Tan temprano? ¿Hoy es día de fiesta?
Marisol: No, siempre se cierra a las dos.
Becky: Entonces, vamos a la farmacia.
Marisol: No lo hay en la farmacia y además está cerrada. Podemos volver más tarde, Becky.
Becky: Este... Quiero escribir unas cartas esta tarde.
Marisol: Te doy papel. Vámonos. Mamá nos espera para la comida.

Why can't Becky buy paper?

A. There really is not time because they are already late for lunch. (Turn to p. 97, A)
B. The stores are closed for lunch. (Turn to p. 65, B)
C. It is a holiday and the stores close early on holidays. (Turn to p. 102, C)
D. Marisol just does not want to be bothered going to the store for one item. (Turn to p. 107, D)

22. El indígena

Cuzco, Perú

Alfredo: No sé si ésta es la calle que va a la estación o no.
Steve: ¿No has estado aquí en Cuzco antes?
Alfredo: Sí, una vez de vacaciones hace unos cinco años. Pero no me acuerdo bien de ° la ciudad.
Steve: Entonces, preguntemos a alguien. Aquí viene un hombre. Señor, ¿puede decirme dónde está la estación del ferrocarril?
Alfredo: Este hombre es indígena.
Steve: Señor, queremos ir a la estación de donde salen los trenes. ¿Sabe usted dónde está?
Alfredo: Steve, es indio. Solamente sabe quechua.
Steve: Señor, ¿cómo se llama esta calle?
Alfredo: No va a contestar, Steve. Bueno, creo que reconozco esta bocacalle.° La estación está a la derecha.
Steve: Al menos el hombre debe tener un poco de cortesía.

Why didn't the man answer them?

A. The man is deaf and dumb. (Turn to p. 107, A)
B. The man is also a stranger in Cuzco. (Turn to p. 88, B)
C. The man does not speak Spanish. (Turn to p. 60, C)
D. The man is an Indian and they do not speak to strangers in public. (Turn to p. 101, D)

---

no me acuerdo de I don't remember   **bocacalle** intersection

23. Playas y poesías

Betsy está pasando las vacaciones con los Marín, una familia cubano-americana, Miami, Florida.

Betsy: El clima de Florida es maravilloso. Hace calor en diciembre. Imagínate una noche tan calurosa en Michigan en diciembre. ¡Qué hermosa es esta playa!°

Tomás: Nunca la he visto pero se dice que la nieve° es muy hermosa también.

Betsy: Eso sí que es, pero hace mucho frío. Yo prefiero un clima más templado.

Tomás: Pues, he leído la poesía de Robert Frost y me gusta mucho. Me gustaría ver un bosque° cuando nieva.

Betsy: Tengo frío solamente de pensar en la nieve. Y, ¡Robert Frost! Hasta su nombre me da frío. ¡Vamos a hablar de la playa, el mar, el sol!

Tomás: Bueno, no te gusta Robert Frost, pero sí te gustaría José María Heredia. «Yo te amo,,Sol: Tú sabes cuán gozoso,° cuando en las puertas del oriente° asomas° siempre te saludé.»

Betsy: ¿Es un poema?

Tomás: Sí, pero no vamos a hablar del clima. Vamos a hablar de ti. ¿Qué es poesía? ¿Y tú me lo preguntas? Poesía... eres tú.

Betsy: Pues... Gracias. ¿Eres buen estudiante de la literatura?

Tomás: Ay, no me menciones la escuela. Estamos de vacaciones.

Betsy: Claro, pero es tarde. Debemos regresar a tu casa, ¿no? Mañana tú me enseñas el esquí acuático.

Tomás: Sí, regresamos, pero nos paseamos muy lentamente de regreso. ¿Conoces el poema «Romance de la luna, luna»?

Why does Tomás keep talking about poetry?

A. Literature is the favorite subject of many Latin Americans. (Turn to p. 61, A)

B. Tomás is not a very good conversationalist and cannot think of anything else to talk about. (Turn to p. 101, B)

C. Tomás likes Betsy very much and is being romantic. (Turn to p. 74, C)

D. Tomás is an exceptionally intelligent student. (Turn to p. 106, D)

---

playa	beach	**bosque**	woods	**oriente**	East
nieve	snow	**gozoso**	cheerful	**asomas**	you look out

23

24. ¡Estoy embarazada!

Una tienda de modas, San Juan, Puerto Rico

Dependienta: ¿Puedo servirle?
Linda: Quiero probarme° estos pantalones.
Dependienta: Muy bien, señorita. Para acá, por esta puerta.

(Tres minutos más tarde)

Dependienta: ¿Le quedan° bien?
Linda: Me gustan mucho, pero me quedan muy pequeños.
Dependienta: Un momento, señorita, creo que los tenemos en otro tamaño.° (Sale y regresa inmediatamente.) Aquí los tiene usted.
Linda: Gracias.

(Tres minutos más tarde)

Linda: Estos también me quedan un poco pequeños. Creo que he ganado algún peso.° ¡Estoy embarazada!
Dependienta: ¡Qué bueno! Me alegro. ¡Qué suerte tiene usted! Usted y su marido deben ser muy felices.

Why is the saleswoman so happy about Linda gaining weight?

A. The saleswoman thinks that Linda is expecting a baby. (Turn to p. 98, A)
B. The saleswoman is trying to be nice and to be complimentary so that Linda will buy the slacks. (Turn to p. 64, B)
C. Linda, like many American girls, is fashionably thin. Like many Latin Americans, the saleswoman is glad that she is gaining a little weight. (Turn to p. 83, C)
D. The saleswoman knows that Linda has been ill and is happy that she is better. (Turn to p. 97, D)

---

probarme to try on
quedan do they fit

tamaño size
he ganado peso I have gained weight

25. ¿Qué usar?

Buenos Aires, Argentina

Isabel: Andrés y Emilio quieren salir° con nosotras esta noche.

Marcia: Muy bien. Me gusta mucho salir con ellos. Y ahora tengo una oportunidad de usar mi vestido verde, el nuevo. ¿Adónde vamos?

Isabel: Andrés dice que quiere ir a la Exposición de Ganadería.°

Marcia: ¿La Exposición de Ganadería? ¿Para ver el ganado?°

Isabel: Sí. Es muy interesante. Todos los mejores del país están allí. Son animales formidables. Y también tienen los campeones hípicos.°

Marcia: Bueno, si ustedes tres quieren ir allí, bien. ¿Tienen un parque de diversiones allí también, con un tiovivo° y una montaña rusa?°

Isabel: ¿En la Exposición de Ganadería? No. Esta noche van a premiar° el mejor de la exposición. Y además vemos los saltos° de los caballos.

Marcia: Entonces tengo que lavar mis jeans. Están sucios.

Isabel: ¿Por qué? ¿No vas a usar el vestido nuevo?

Marcia: ¿A la Exposición de Ganadería? ¿No es mejor usar pantalones?

Isabel: Si quieres... posiblemente ese traje de pantalones muy bonito que tienes.

Marcia: Y tú, ¿qué vas a usar?

Isabel: Mi vestido amarillo. Quiero lucirme° esta noche. Muchas veces se ven allí las estrellas del cine o de la televisión. Ponte el vestido verde, Marcia.

Marcia: Pero es nuevo. ¿No debo usar algo menos elegante para la Exposición de Ganadería?

Why doesn't Marcia want to dress up to go to the Cattle Show?

A. Marcia could not ride a horse in a dress. (Turn to p. 71, A)

B. It is like a fair and Marcia would rather wear jeans to a fair. (Turn to p. 89, B)

C. In Latin America, the girls do not wear pantsuits on a date. (Turn to p. 68, C)

D. Marcia does not realize that it is a social affair and that everyone there will be dressed up. (Turn to p. 62, D)

---

salir to go out
ganadería livestock, cattle raising
ganado cattle

hípicos of horses
tiovivo merry-go-round
montaña rusa roller coaster

premiar to award
saltos jumps
lucirme to dress up

25

26. Espera la señorita.

El teatro, Barcelona, España

Dave:	Aquí están los billetes. Fila° 24, asientos 18 y 19.
Bill:	Creo que están por este pasillo° a la derecha.
Dave:	No, a la izquierda. Hay una acomodadora° que puede ayudarnos. Aquí están nuestros billetes, señorita.
Acomodadora:	Por acá, señores. Por el pasillo a la izquierda.
Dave:	Tengo razón.
Acomodadora:	Aquí están los asientos, el tercero y el cuarto.
Dave:	Muchas gracias, señorita. Son asientos muy buenos.
Bill:	Es verdad. Podemos ver la comedia muy bien.
Dave:	Debe ser una comedia muy buena.
Bill:	Sí. ¿Por qué todavía está aquí la acomodadora?
Dave:	¿Estos son nuestros asientos, señorita?
Acomodadora:	Sí, señor.
Dave:	Muchas gracias.
Bill:	Aún está esperando. ¿Tienes los carteles?°
Dave:	Sí, tengo dos.
Bill:	¿Estás seguro de que éstos son nuestros asientos?
Dave:	Claro, ella nos los enseñó.
Bill:	¿Por qué espera?

What is the usher waiting for?

A. The usher expects a tip. (Turn to p. 73, A)
B. The usher thinks they are cute and is hoping they will ask her for her phone number. (Turn to p. 93, B)
C. They forgot to dismiss her. (Turn to p. 100, C)
D. They should be gentlemen and walk her back up the aisle before taking their seats. (Turn to p. 98, D)

---

fila row
pasillo aisle

acomodadora usher
carteles programs

27. Dolor de cabeza

En casa, La Ceiba, Honduras

Amy: ¡Ay de mí! Tengo dolor de cabeza.

Margarita: ¡Qué lástima! ¿Por qué no descansas un rato?

Amy: Buena idea. Pero primero quiero un vaso de agua muy fría. Tengo mucho calor.

Margarita: ¡Tienes fiebre! No debes tomar nada frío. No es bueno para el cuerpo.

Amy: No, creo que no tengo fiebre. Es que hace mucho calor y estaba jugando al tenis con Mario. No es nada más que un dolor de cabeza.

Margarita: Sin embargo, debes tomar algo, una limonada caliente con dos aspirinas.

Amy: ¡Una limonada caliente! No, gracias, pero sí, voy a tomar las aspirinas y descansar un rato.

Margarita: Pues, no pongas hielo° en el agua. Posiblemente tienes dolor de cabeza porque siempre tomas las bebidas tan frías. El frío te da un dolor de cabeza y también te puede dar un resfriado.

Amy: Bueno, tengo calor, tengo dolor de cabeza, tengo sed, y por eso tengo ganas de tomar un vaso de agua fría. Además, Margarita, yo estoy acostumbrada a tomar el agua así.

Margarita: Pues, todavía creo yo que no es buena idea. Pero, de veras, espero que te mejores° pronto.

Amy: Gracias, Margarita. Y ahora voy a descansar un rato.

Why doesn't Margarita want Amy to drink cold water?

A. The ice cubes are not made from purified water. (Turn to p. 65, A)

B. Margarita thinks Amy should cool off gradually after playing tennis. (Turn to p. 77, B)

C. Margarita is upset because Amy does not want to try her hot lemonade. (Turn to p. 94, C)

D. Margarita thinks that iced drinks are bad for people, especially people who do not feel well. (Turn to p. 75, D)

---

hielo ice   **te mejores** you get better

27

28. Dolor de espalda

En casa, La Ceiba, Honduras

Margarita:	¿Cómo te sientes ahora?
Amy:	No tengo dolor de cabeza tan fuerte, pero ahora me duele la espalda. Me gusta jugar al tenis pero, ¿por qué jugué tres horas? ¡Qué tonta estoy a veces!
Margarita:	¿La espalda también? Eso es serio. Voy a decírselo a mamá.
Amy:	No. Estoy segura de que no es nada.
Margarita:	Mamá, Amy todavía tiene dolor de cabeza, y también le duele la espalda.
Mamá:	Posiblemente está mala del hígado.° Yo tengo unas pastillas° muy buenas. Muchas veces cuando le duele la espalda, es el hígado. Y voy a llamar al médico.
Amy:	Por favor, no te molestes.° Mañana voy a estar perfectamente bien. No es necesario llamar al médico.
Papá:	¿Qué pasa? ¿Quién está enferma?
Mamá:	Amy no se siente bien. Le duelen la cabeza y la espalda.
Papá:	¿De veras? Puede ser la gripe. He oído que hay muchos enfermos ahora con la gripe.
Amy:	No, no. No estoy enferma. Estuve jugando al tenis con Mario esta tarde casi tres horas al sol. Por eso me duelen la cabeza y la espalda. Casi tengo miedo decirlo pero también me duele el brazo derecho. Pero, es el tenis, nada más.
Papá:	Puede ser, pero llamamos al médico de todos modos.°

What is wrong with Amy?

A. Amy is a hypochondriac and she *thinks* something is wrong. (Turn to p. 100, A)
B. Amy has a headache and sore muscles. (Turn to p. 60, B)
C. Amy is coming down with the flu. (Turn to p. 81, C)
D. Amy has a bad liver. (Turn to p. 79, D)

---

hígado liver
pastillas pills

no te molestes don't bother
de todos modos anyhow

29. Margaritas y rosas

El dos de julio, la casa de los Císneros, La Paz, Bolivia

Joan: Me gusta mucho tu casa. Es muy bonita y muy moderna.
Lucía: Gracias. Me alegro de que estés contenta aquí.
Joan: Claro que sí. Me gustan también todas las flores en la casa. ¡Qué amable saludarme con las rosas tan bonitas!
Lucía: Papá trae más hoy. Aquí viene. Hola, papá.
Papá: Hola, Lucía. Buenas tardes, Joan. ¿Cómo estás? Te traigo unas flores.
Joan: ¿Más flores?
Papá: Lucía, llama a Lola que traiga dos floreros.°
Lucía: Sí, papá. A Joan le gustan las flores. Lola... Lola...
Papá: ¿Qué te gustan más, los claveles° o los lirios?°
Joan: Creo que los claveles. Pero, ¿por qué...?
Papá: Muy bien. Para ti, los claveles y para la sala, los lirios.
Lucía: ¿Y para mí?
Papá: Bueno, mañana voy a comprar más. ¿Qué quieres que compre?
Lucía: Yo prefiero las margaritas.°
Joan: ¿Mañana, otra vez? No lo creo.
Lucía: Y papá, a Joan le gustan las rosas también.
Papá: Está bien. Mañana, margaritas y rosas.
Joan: ¡Qué ricos son ustedes! Dos criadas y flores todos los días.

Why are there so many flowers in the house?

A. Flowers are given for special events. They got some for Joan who just arrived, and now they are getting ready for a holiday. (Turn to p. 67, A)
B. In the summertime there are often many flowers in the house. (Turn to p. 92, B)
C. The Císneros are wealthy and can afford to have many flowers. (Turn to p. 98, C)
D. Latin Americans are accustomed to having flowers in the house and most families often have fresh flowers. (Turn to p. 85, D)

---

floreros vases
claveles carnations

lirios lilies, irises
margaritas daisies

30. Pesos y dólares

La Ciudad de México, México

Sandy:	Mira esta revista. La quiero. ¿Qué precio tiene?
Emilia:	Creo que trenta y cinco pesos. Es una telenovela° y éstas no cuestan mucho. Yo voy a comprar una también, ésa de la nueva serie. Todavía tenemos noventa pesos. (Al vendedor) ¡Psst! ¿Cuánto le debemos por estas dos?
Vendedor:	Setenta pesos, señorita. Les doy tres por noventa pesos.
Emilia:	No, gracias. Necesitamos veinte pesos para el pesero.°
(Más tarde)	
Sandy:	¿Cuánto cuesta la revista en dólares?
Emilia:	No estoy segura. Creo que un cuarto de un dólar.
Sandy:	Me sorprende. No cuesta mucho en dinero verdadero.
Emilia:	Es lo mismo que cuesta en pesos.
Sandy:	Pero, cuesta trenta y cinco pesos y es solamente veinticinco centavos. Es porque nuestro dinero vale más.
Emilia:	No vale más. Un peso vale 0,7 de un centavo. Hay unos ciento cuarenta y cinco pesos en cada dólar. Un dólar vale ciento cuarenta y cinco. El precio es igual en pesos o en dólares.
Sandy:	¿Por que hay 145 en un dólar? Es muy dificil cambiar el dinero así. ¿Tienen un billete° de ciento cuarenta y cinco?
Emilia:	Claro que no. Tenemos billetes de 50, 100, 500 y 1000.
Sandy:	Pero, ¿cien pesos? Entonces ustedes tienen un billete de setenta centavos. ¿Por que?
Emilia:	¡Sandy! ¡Nuestro dinero es el dinero de México! Voy a pedir que papá te explique esto.

Why doesn't Sandy understand Mexican money?

A. Sandy was not very good at math and cannot figure out how much Mexican money is worth. (Turn to p. 83, A)
B. Mexican money has a different numerical system, like the English pounds, shillings and sixpence used to be. (Turn to p. 69, B)
C. Sandy does not really understand the concept of money, not just Mexican money. She would have the same difficulties in France, Germany, etc. (Turn to p. 61, C)
D. Things are usually cheaper in Mexico so the dollar is worth more. (Turn to p. 88, D)

---

telenovela pictorialized novel   **billete** bill (paper money)
pesero taxi with a fixed route

31. Hola, Flaquita

San José, Costa Rica

Gloria: Mamá, este arroz con pollo está delicioso.
Mamá: Gracias. Beth, ¿quieres más pollo?
Beth: No, estoy a dieta.
Mamá: ¿A dieta? ¿Necesitas comida especial? Puedo prepararte lo que necesites. ¿Puedes comer bisté?
Beth: Sí, puedo comerlo, pero no quiero comer mucho.
Papá: ¿Has estado enferma, Beth?
Beth: No, es que quiero perder peso.
Gloria: ¿Perder peso? Pero, Beth, eres muy delgada.

(Más tarde llega Pablo.)

Pablo: Hola, Flaquita, ¿cómo estás?
Beth: Estoy muy bien, gracias.
Pablo: Entonces, ¿quieren ustedes ir a la fuente de sodas para tomar algo?
Gloria: ¡Qué buena idea! Yo quiero un batido° de chocolate.
Beth: Me gustaría ir, pero no voy a tomar nada.
Pablo: Sí, tú necesitas tomar algo. Pareces hambrienta, chica.
Beth: No, acabamos de comer hace una hora.

Why does everyone want Beth to eat more?

A. Although Beth may be fashionably thin by North American standards, she is too thin for a Latin American. (Turn to p. 62, A)
B. Beth has been ill and they want her to regain her health. (Turn to p. 98, B)
C. It is polite to offer guests something to eat. (Turn to p. 101, C)
D. Beth is really overweight and everyone assumes that she eats too much. (Turn to p. 57, D)

---

perder peso to lose weight   **batido** milk shake

32.   Y yo sin frenos

El Parque del Buen Retiro, Madrid

Lynn:	¡Qué bonito día! ¡Y qué parque más bonito!
Chavela:	Claro. Mira las flores. Me gustan las rosas.
Joven:	¡Ay, chicas! ¡Qué suerte tengo de ver unas tan guapas!
Lynn:	Chavela, ¿quién es ese muchacho?
Chavela:	No sé.
Joven:	Eres una rosa divina, y tú, una flor exquisita.
Chavela:	Tienes un pretendiente.°
Lynn:	Pero yo no lo conozco.
Joven:	Tantas curvas y yo sin frenos.°
Lynn:	¡Qué molestia! No me gusta ese tipo.
Chavela:	Sí que es un tipo, pero muy agradable, ¿no?
Joven:	Me muero de ansia.°
Lynn:	¡No! Chavela, yo no lo conozco. Mejor será que nos vayamos.
Chavela:	¿Por qué? Es un día magnífico y me gusta pasear por el parque.
Lynn:	Pues, ese muchacho nos está siguiendo. ¡No puedo más!°

What is bothering Lynn?

A. Lynn is in a bad mood, because on such a nice day, she does not want to just walk in the park. (Turn to p. 86, A)
B. Lynn is annoyed with Chavela for not introducing her although the boy obviously knows Chavela. (Turn to p. 108, B)
C. The boy is making rude remarks which Lynn does not like. (Turn to p. 65, C)
D. Lynn is annoyed because she thinks the boy is getting fresh and has a lot of nerve following them. (Turn to p. 83, D)

---

pretendiente suitor
frenos brakes

ansia longing
no puedo más I can't stand it anymore

33. Mañana, sí

El lunes en la tienda de Kodak, Caracas, Venezuela

Bob: Mi cámara está descompuesta.
Dependiente: Bueno, la reparamos.
Bob: ¿Cuándo estará lista?
Dependiente: El miércoles, señor.
Bob: Regreso entonces.

(El jueves)

Bob: ¿Está lista mi cámara?
Dependiente: No, señor. Todavía no está terminada. Regrese usted mañana. Estará lista.
Bob: Regresé ayer y regreso hoy. ¡Ay de mí! ¿Cuántas veces más tengo que regresar?
Dependiente: Pues, señor, es que hay mucho trabajo esta semana. Mañana la tendré reparada para usted.
Bob: ¿Sin falta?
Dependiente: No se preocupe. Mañana, sí.

What does Bob still have to learn about Latin Americans?

A. Many Latin American nations are underdeveloped in terms of technological achievements. Thus, repairing such items as cameras and appliances causes many problems. (Turn to p. 106, A)
B. Latin Americans often politely tell you what you want to hear. (Turn to p. 95, B)
C. Latin Americans do not like to admit their faults. (Turn to p. 109, C)
D. Putting things off until *mañana* is typical of Latin Americans. (Turn to p. 73, D)

34. Las bodas

Guayaquil, Ecuador

Josefina: ¿Quieres ir conmigo esta tarde? Fernando y Anita van a casarse.

Mary Lou: ¿Fernando, tu hermano mayor?

Josefina: Sí. La ceremonia no dura mucho tiempo. Estoy segura de que tenemos bastante tiempo para ver esa película nueva en el Cine Bolívar.

Mary Lou: Tu papá todavía está de negocios en el Brasil. ¿No aprueban tus padres de su matrimonio?

Josefina: Claro que sí, pero regresa el sábado, una semana antes de la boda.°

Mary Lou: Tú dijiste que la boda iba a ser esta tarde.

Josefina: Sí, pero es la ceremonia civil, nada más. Mi primo Antonio y yo somos los testigos.° Por eso me es necesario ir.

Mary Lou: Yo creía que la hermana de Anita iba a ser la madrina de bodas.°

Josefina: Sí, pero como vive en Quito, no viene hoy. Va a llegar la semana que viene.

Mary Lou: Entonces la boda es el domingo de la semana que viene, ¿verdad?

Josefina: Claro. Bueno, ¿vas conmigo esta tarde al Palacio Municipal para la ceremonia?

When is the wedding?

A. There are two weddings. Fernando and Anita's is today and Anita's sister's is a week from Sunday. (Turn to p. 103, A)
B. They are just getting the license today and the wedding is a week from Sunday. (Turn to p. 75, B)
C. The ceremony is today and the family celebration is a week from Sunday. (Turn to p. 95, C)
D. There are two ceremonies. The civil ceremony is today and the religious ceremony is a week from Sunday. (Turn to p. 72, D)

---

boda wedding
testigos witnesses

madrina de bodas bridesmaid

35. En el mercado

El Mercado Libertad, Guadalajara, México

Karen: Mira, Luisa, esa bolsa amarilla. ¡Qué bonita es! Me gustaría comprarla para mi hermana. ¿Cuánto costará?

Luisa: Probablemente muy poco. La vendedora tiene muchas.

Karen: (Hablando a la vendedora) ¿Qué precio tiene esta bolsa amarilla?

Vendedora: Para usted, señorita, solamente setecientos pesos.

Karen: ¿Solamente setecientos pesos? ¿Cuatro dólares, noventa centavos? Luisa, tienes razón, es muy barata. Entonces, voy a comprarla. Aquí tiene los setecientos pesos. ¡Qué feliz será mi hermana!

Luisa: Pero, Karen, ¡setecientos pesos es mucho por la bolsa! ¿Por qué la compras? Ese precio es ridículo. Es porque tú eres norteamericana.

Karen: No, ese precio no es mucho por una bolsa así.

Luisa: Sí, lo es. Bueno, vámonos pues.

Do you know why Luisa disapproves of Karen buying the purse?

A. It is really a cheap purse and Luisa does not want Karen to get the wrong idea of Mexican products. (Turn to p. 96, A)

B. Luisa is jealous that Karen has enough money to buy the purse. (Turn to p. 97, B)

C. At a market in Mexico it is the custom to bargain and Karen accepted the first price mentioned without bargaining. (Turn to p. 89, C)

D. Karen tried to pay for the purse with U.S. money. (Turn to p. 93, D)

36. Los americanos son ricos.

La casa de los Ordóñez, Guadalajara, México

Luisa: Mamá, Karen compró una bolsa en el mercado a setecientos pesos y solamente vale cuatrocientos.
Mamá: Pues, la vendedora puso ese precio porque es nor-
teamericana. Y tú, ¿no le dijiste nada?
Luisa: Sí, mamá, pero Karen no me escuchó. Ella dijo que era
barata. Todos los norteamericanos tienen mucho dinero,
¿verdad?
Mamá: No es verdad, pero es cierto que no saben comprar.
Luisa: Y más tarde ella quiso ir en un pesero y cuando bajamos,
¡le dio al chofer una propina° de un peso extra!
Mamá: Tenemos que hacerle comprender lo que es un pesero.
Ella probablemente creyó que era un taxi.
Luisa: Pues, de todos modos, Karen es rica. Siempre tiene
mucho dinero.

**Why does Luisa think that all North Americans have a lot of
money?**

A. It is true that all North Americans have more money in compari-
son to Mexicans. (Turn to p. 92, A)
B. Americans find it difficult to judge how much an item or a
service is worth in another country and often pay higher prices
that a native would. (Turn to p. 83, B)
C. Americans do not bargain; therefore they must have more
money to pay the higher prices that are asked first. (Turn to
p. 85, C)
D. Dollars are worth more than pesos. (Turn to p. 87, D)

---

propina tip

37. Te quiero, Ruffy

La casa de los Smith, Chicago, Ill.

Diane:	Hola, Jack. Entra. Aquí estamos en la sala.
Jack:	Hola. ¿Cómo están?
Maribel:	Diane, ¡entró también el perro!
Diane:	Sí. ¡Ven acá Ruffy! ¡Qué buen perro!
Jack:	¡Atta boy, Ruffy! ¿No es un animal magnífico, Maribel?
Maribel:	Bueno, puede ser magnífico, pero...
Diane:	Para acá, Ruffy. Levántate. Te doy de comer. Muy bien. Ay, cómo te quiero, Ruffy.
Jack:	Quisiera que me dijeras eso a mí. Pero tienes razón. Ruffy se porta° muy bien, mejor que mi hermanito.
Maribel:	¿Ruffy es como un sereno?° ¿Cómo perro guardián?
Diane:	No, Maribel. Ruffy quiere a todos. (Riéndose) Creo que hasta a los ladrones.
Maribel:	¿Un perro dentro de la casa? Nunca voy a entender a ustedes los norteamericanos.

What doesn't Maribel understand?

A. Ruffy is very ugly and the American young people are putting up a fuss over what might be called a mutt. (Turn to p. 105, A)

B. Cats and birds are the favored animals in Latin America. Maribel does not understand that dogs are also favorites here. (Turn to p. 102, B)

C. Usually only the night watchmen have dogs in Latin America. (Turn to p. 79, C)

D. Latin Americans do not usually think of animals as «pets.» (Turn to p. 78, D)

---

se porta behaves   **sereno** watchman

38. ¿Lobo, Monstruo o Ben?

Córdoba, Argentina

Sr. Lombardi: ¡Estela! Ven acá. Pablito, Carmelita, Rosana, Grace, ¡vengan!

Sra. Lombardi: Ricardo, ¿qué pasa? ¿Por qué nos llamas? (Ve el perro.) Ricardo, nos traes otro perro.

Pablito: ¡Papá! ¡Un perrito! ¿Es mío? Yo lo quiero.

Carmelita: No, papá. Es para mí. Pablito tiene Nube.

Sr. Lombardi: Nube es el perro de toda la familia. Pero es bastante viejo y hoy día con los problemas del gobierno, necesitamos mejor protección. Aunque es pequeño ahora, miren ustedes lo grande que son las patas.° Será un perro formidable.

Grace: ¿Cuál es su nombre?

Sr. Lombardi: Todavía no tiene nombre. ¿Tienes sugerencias?

Grace: ¡Fernando! Se parece mucho a Fernando Lorenzo, ¿no crees?, con el pelo sobre los ojos. O Tomás. Mi hermanito en los Estados Unidos se llama Tommy y aunque es pequeño, parece que va a ser grande como mi papá.

Sra. Lombardi: ¡Qué chistosa eres! Pero esos nombres no son buenos para el perro.

Rosana: Serían buenos nombres Lobo o Monstruo.

Grace: Nuestro se llama Benjamin Peter Dog the Third.

Sr. Lombardi: ¿De veras? Es un nombre muy curioso. ¿Dices Benjamín? ¿Pedro?

Grace: Sí, pero lo llamamos Ben.

Sra. Lombardi: ¡Qué raro! Pues no debemos usar ese nombre.

Grace: ¿Charlie?

Pablito: Yo sé. Es Pirata Primero.

Carmelita: Sí, papá. Pirata. Llámalo Pirata I.

Sra. Lombardi: Me parece muy bien.

Sr. Lombardi: Entonces, estamos de acuerdo. Se llama Pirata I.

Pablito: Ven, Pirata.

Why didn't the family like any of Grace's suggestions?

A. The names are all American. (Turn to p. 109, A)

B. They are all saints' names. (Turn to p. 70, B)

C. A member of their own family should name him. (Turn to p. 107, C)

D. The names are too tame for a watchdog. (Turn to p. 108, D)

---

patas paws

39. La farmacia

Durante el descanso, en la escuela Reina de los Ángeles, Lima, Perú

Mary Jo: Oye, Meche, vamos al centro esta tarde. Necesito maquillaje.°

Meche: Muy bien. Y yo quiero comprar un peine.°

Mary Jo: Entonces nos vemos después. Hasta luego.

(Más tarde en el centro)

Meche: ¿A qué hora tienes que estar en casa?

Mary Jo: A las siete. El tío Roberto viene a comer con nosotros esta noche.

Meche: Entonces tenemos tiempo, casi dos horas.

Mary Jo: Allí está la farmacia. Vámonos.

Meche: ¿Qué vas a comprar en la farmacia? ¿Necesitas medicina?

Mary Jo: No. Necesito más maquillaje. También quiero comprar una tarjeta.°

Meche: No, chica. No los hay.

Mary Jo: Pues, no me importa la marca.° No es necesario comprar maquillaje norteamericano.

Meche: En la farmacia no hay nada. Vamos a la tienda Novedades.

Mary Jo: Pero la farmacia está cerca. Compremos las cosas necesarias aquí, y entonces tenemos tiempo para ir de tienda en tienda.

Meche: Pero si no necesitas medicina, ¿para qué ir a la farmacia?

Why doesn't Meche want to go to the drugstore?

A. Because they do not sell makeup and postcards at the drugstore in Latin America. They do sell medicine and health products. (Turn to p. 76, A)

B. Meche prefers to look around the department store since they have time. (Turn to p. 104, B)

C. Latin Americans do not like to think about being ill, so they avoid drugstores unless absolutely necessary. (Turn to p. 103, C)

D. The drugstores do not carry North American products. which Meche prefers. (Turn to p. 95, D)

---

maquillaje makeup
peine comb

tarjeta card
marca brand

40. ¡Dios mío!

La Avenida Insurgentes, México, D. F.

María: ¡Dios mío! ¡Ese tráfico es increíble! No vamos a llegar a tiempo.

Judy: Ay, María. No debes decir eso.

María: Pues, es verdad. Insurgentes tiene el peor tráfico de toda la ciudad. ¡Por Dios! Ese bendito° pesero casi se me chocó.°

Judy: No es eso. Estoy de acuerdo con que el tráfico es pesado, pero no te enojes° tanto que....

María: ¿Tú ves ese cochino° camión? ¿Por qué no dejé que Manuel manejara como quisiera? ¡Dios me ayude!

Judy: Ay, María, ese lenguaje. Mi mamá no me permite que hable así yo.

What is wrong with what María is saying?

A. Mexican women usually do not show that they are angry or upset. Judy is surprised at what María is saying. (Turn to p. 79, A)

B. María should be paying attention to her driving instead of talking. (Turn to p. 91, B)

C. María keeps saying *Dios* and Judy knows that María's mother wants her to be ladylike when she speaks and to use good Spanish. (Turn to p. 99, C)

D. Nothing is wrong. María has not said anything that is not correct for a Mexican girl to say. (Turn to p. 61, D)

---

bendito blessed
chocó hit, collided

no te enojes don't get angry
cochino darn

40

41. La mamá de Vicente

Caey, Puerto Rico

Phil:	Me agrada mucho la oportunidad de pasar las vacaciones aquí en Puerto Rico con tu familia. Ustedes son muy amables.
Vicente:	Gracias. Esperamos que disfrutes mucho de tu visita.
Phil:	Una cosa que me gusta mucho es la comida.
Vicente:	Seguro. Vas a ganar cinco kilos o más, chico.
Phil:	Tu madre...
Vicente:	Mi mamá es una cocinera muy buena, ¿verdad?
Phil:	Claro que sí. Tu madre...
Vicente:	¡No digas eso! Mi mamá es una buena mujer.
Phil:	¿Por qué te enojas? Ella es muy simpática y además va a enseñarme a preparar plátanos fritos.
Vicente:	Hombre, ¿tú quieres aprender a cocinar?
Phil:	Ya sé cocinar. Es una afición° conmigo. Y tu madre...
Vicente:	Phil, ¡no debes hablar así de mi mamá!
Phil:	Pero ella entiende que en Ohio hay muchos hombres a quienes les gusta cocinar. El cocinar es un arte.
Vicente:	No es eso. Aquí no hablamos así de las mujeres.
Phil:	Yo sé que las mujeres aquí tienen criadas para ayudar, pero tu madre dice que...
Vicente:	¡Dios mío! ¡No puedo más!

Why is Vicente angry?

A. Vicente does not want Phil to talk about his mother being a cook. (Turn to p. 58, A)
B. Phil should not say *tu madre*. (Turn to p. 62, B)
C. Phil should not admit he can cook. That is women's work. (Turn to p. 69, C)
D. Vicente is on a diet and does not want to talk about cooking. (Turn to p. 103, D)

---

afición interest, hobby

42. ¿Más fotos?

El parque, Caracas, Venezuela

Rich: ¡Ah!, ésta es una vista tremenda. Momentito. Quiero sacar una foto. ¿Dónde estará la cámara?
Carlos: Probablemente está en el coche. Pero, Rich, vamos a ver los animales.
Rich: Okay, voy muy rápidamente por la cámara. (Sale corriendo.)
Mario: Ese chico se vuelve loco sacando fotos. Debe haber sacado cien fotos esta semana.
Carlos: Por lo menos. Siempre se las manda en las cartas a sus amigos. Es posible que lo haga para ellos pero, ¡tantas!
Rich: Tengo la cámara. La encontré en el coche. Quiero sacar una foto de los jardines, aaaaaquí... y una de la fuente... y una más de ustedes enfrente de la entrada... Gracias. Y...
Carlos: Oye, ahora al jardín zoológico, ¿eh?
Mario: De acuerdo. Es hora de encontrarnos con las chicas.
Rich: Allí están los monos.° ¡Qué foto más cómica será ésta!
Mario: ¿Otra vez? Tú siempre estás sacando fotos, chico. ¿Ya no tienes suficiente?
Rich: Tengo bastante, pero... solamente una más.
Carlos: ¡Ay, no! ¡Chico! Belita y Juana nos esperan.

Why do Carlos and Mario think that Rich should not take so many pictures?

A. Taking many pictures is an activity that interests North Americans. Latin Americans take pictures but only a limited number. (Turn to p. 72, A)
B. The boys will be late meeting the girls. (Turn to p. 82, B)
C. Taking so many pictures is slowing them down and they have many other things to do. (Turn to p. 77, C)
D. Latin Americans do not like to have pictures taken of their country. (Turn to p. 68, D)

---

monos monkeys

43. Los libros

En un ómnibus, Montevideo, Uruguay

Ron: ¿Tenemos tiempo esta tarde antes de ir a casa? Tengo que bajarme en la Avenida 18 de Julio.

Gerardo: ¿Por qué? ¿Quieres ir al cine?

Ron: Ojalá pudiera. Pero lo que tengo que hacer es comprar unos libros para la clase de literatura rioplatense.° Es imposible sacarlos de la biblioteca.

Gerardo: Sí, tenemos tiempo. ¿Qué tienes que comprar?

Ron: De la Argentina, José Hernández y...

Gerardo: Muy bien. Vas a leer *Martín Fierro*.

Ron: Sí, y Jorge Luis Borges y Marco Denevi.

Gerardo: Te va a gustar mucho Marco Denevi. Es moderno y sus cuentos son muy cortos.

Ron: Del Paraguay, solamente Herib Campos Cervera, y del Uruguay, Juana de Ibarbourou y Horacio Quiroga.

Gerardo: También te va a gustar Horacio Quiroga. Bueno, vamos a la Librería Presidente. Tiene de todo.

(Más tarde)

Gerardo: ¡Cuatro libros! ¡Cuánto vas a estudiar!

Ron: Sí, pero no tengo que leer todo el libro más grande. ¡Ay, no! Mira este libro de Quiroga. No se han cortado las páginas. ¿Hay tiempo para regresar a la librería?

Gerardo: ¿Te has olvidado de algo?

Ron: No, pero este libro no está bueno. No puedo separar las páginas.

Gerardo: Está bien. Las cortamos en casa.

Ron: Pero yo pagué un buen precio por este libro. Si no hay un descuento, quiero un libro bueno.

Gerardo: Este libro es bueno. Ah, aquí viene el ómnibus. Vámonos.

Ron: Pero, ¿qué vamos a hacer con el libro?

Why isn't Gerardo upset about the book with the uncut pages?

A. It is not his book. (Turn to p. 63, A)

B. Latin Americans do not expect everything to be absolutely perfect. (Turn to p. 74, B)

C. Many books in Latin America, especially paperbacks, come with uncut pages. (Turn to p. 57, C)

D. Gerardo does not want to make a fuss at the bookstore because a friend of his father is the owner. (Turn to p. 90, D)

---

rioplatense from the Río de la Plata area

44. Cambiando la llanta

Un camino, San Diego, California

Nacho: Oye, Dick, ¿qué estás haciendo con el coche?
Dick: Se me bajó una llanta° y la estoy cambiando.
Nacho: Pero, ese trabajo es bastante sucio. ¿No hay un garaje cerca?
Dick: No vale la pena. Es fácil cambiarla y además, afortunadamente me visto de ropa de sport.
Nacho: ¿No tienes otras cosas más importantes que hacer? Mañana hay un examen de biología, ¿no?
Dick: Bueno, estoy casi terminando. ¿Quieres ir conmigo?
Nacho: Por supuesto, pero ojalá que no se nos baje otra llanta.
Dick: Es una posibilidad. Esas llantas son bastante viejas. Pero, si ocurre, la cambio. Así es la vida.
Nacho: Increíble. Ustedes los norteamericanos son infatigables.

What has impressed Nacho about Dick changing the tire?

A. Dick is still a teenager but is allowed to change tires. A teenager would not be trusted to work on a car in Latin America. (Turn to p. 81, A)
B. Nacho is impressed by the fact that Dick himself is changing the tire. People who have the money to own cars would not normally be changing their own tires. (Turn to p. 59, B)
C. Nacho, like many Latin Americans, is of smaller stature and it seems as though he would not have enough strength to change a tire. (Turn to p. 63, C)
D. Latin Americans take especially good care of their clothes and Nacho does not want Dick to get his clothes dirty, even if they are sport clothes. (Turn to p. 69, D)

---

se... llanta I got a flat tire

45. ¿Quién paga?

Tomando refrescos, San Juan, Puerto Rico

Debbie: Julio, ya son las seis y yo tengo que estar en casa a las seis y media. Siento mucho tener que irme porque esta conversación es interesantísima, pero tía Amelia viene a cenar esta noche.

Julio: Entiendo, Debbie. Tú eres visitante aquí y tienes que cumplir con eso. Pero, puede que continuemos mañana, digamos a las tres. ¿Quieres?

Debbie: Encantada. Ahí viene el camarero. Oiga, la cuenta,° por favor.

Julio: ¡No, no! Vete, Debbie. Ya es tarde.

Debbie: Primero tenemos que pagar.

Julio: Yo lo hago.

Debbie: Pues, entonces, aquí tienes un dólar. Si no es bastante, te pago mañana.

Julio: No, no lo acepto, chica.

Debbie: Julio, yo tengo dinero. Insisto en pagar mi propia cuenta.

Julio: Yo pago y ya no hablemos más de eso.

Debbie: Entonces, mañana me toca a mí.° Yo pagaré la tuya mañana.

Julio: Yo pago mañana también. No te habría invitado si no pudiera pagar. Es mi deber.°

Debbie: Pero, Julio, no permito que siempre pagues tú.

Julio: Aquí pago yo y si no sales ahora mismo, vas a llegar muy tarde.

Why does Julio insist on paying?

A. It is the custom for the male to pay and it would not be honorable for Julio to let Debbie pay. (Turn to p. 68, A)
B. Julio is rich. (Turn to p. 109, B)
C. Not all Puerto Ricans are poor and Julio is trying to show Debbie that this stereotype is wrong. (Turn to p. 67, C)
D. Julio knows that Debbie is in a hurry and wants to be polite. (Turn to p. 104, D)

---

cuenta check   **me toca a mí** it is my turn   **deber** duty

46. Me toca a mí

En casa de los Díaz, Bogotá, Colombia

Jeff: Mi padre me mandó un cheque por mi cumpleaños.

Alonso: ¡Qué suerte, chico! Casi se me olvidó de que tu cumpleaños es mañana. Pero este año celebramos tu santo también.

Jeff: Ojalá que mi padre me mande otro cheque, ¿eh?

Alonso: ¡Qué gracioso! Pero, en serio, ¿quieres ir al banco?

Jeff: Claro que sí. Además quiero ir al correo.

(En el banco)

Jeff: ¡Cuánta gente! ¿Adónde voy para cambiar el cheque?

Guardia: Allí a la ventanilla a la izquierda.

Jeff: Gracias. (Va a la ventanilla.) Hmmm. Pero, ¿dónde está la cola?°

Alonso: Dale el cheque al cajero.°

Jeff: Ese hombre estaba aquí antes.

Alonso: Sí, pero está esperando. Dale el cheque.

Jeff: Ah, ¿qué es eso? Ese hombre se metió enfrente de mí. Creo que me toca a mí.

Alonso: Dale el cheque, hombre. Hay otras cosas que hacer.

Jeff: Pues nadie está turnando. No tienen cortesía. ¿Es ésta la cola?

Alonso: Jeff, ¿por qué no le das el cheque? Yo lo hago por ti.

Jeff: Gracias. ¡Pero ojalá que mi padre no me mande otro cheque! No me gusta el banco.

What hasn't Jeff learned yet?

A. Jeff has not learned that the idea of waiting in line does not always apply under the same circumstances as it does here. (Turn to p. 101, A)

B. Jeff has not learned to get along in crowds and he is still hesitant to do anything with people watching him. (Turn to p. 96, B)

C. Jeff has not learned that people are not going to wait on him just because he is a North American with money. (Turn to p. 75, C)

D. Jeff has not learned that you do not go to a bank to cash a check in Latin America, but rather to the post office. (Turn to p. 66, D)

---

cola line   **cajero** cashier

47. ¿Pagar o no pagar?

Una calle, la una de la mañana, San Jose, Costa Rica

Diego:	¿Dónde está el coche? Allí está.
John:	¡Ay, no! ¿Qué es ese papel?
Diego:	¡Por Dios! Es una noticia de infracción. Nos estacionamos en una zona prohibida. ¿Dónde está el guardia? ¿Lo ves?
John:	No, no veo a nadie.
Diego:	¡Qué chasco!° Es mucho más fácil dar la mordida° al guardia que arreglarlo con el tránsito.°
John:	¿Puedes pagar la multa° al guardia?
Diego:	No, no voy a pagar la multa. Bueno, vamos a casa. El jefe es el compadre de mi tío. Lo llamo mañana.

(Al día siguiente en el teléfono)

Diego:	Quiero hablar con el Sr. Cárdenas Medina.
Recepcionista:	¿De parte de quién?
Diego:	Su sobrino, Jaime Cárdenas Rivera.
Recepcionista:	Un momento, por favor.
Sr. Cárdenas:	¿Diego? ¿En qué puedo servirte?
Diego:	Tío Ricardo, es que ayer John y yo nos estacionamos cerca del Edificio Darío y nos dieron una noticia de infracción. Parece que estábamos estacionados en una zona prohibida. Había muchos otros coches allí y no notamos ningún letrero.°
Sr. Cárdenas:	No te preocupes, Diego. Guillermo Contreras, el Jefe de Tránsito, es mi compadre. Lo llamo ahora.
Diego:	Muchísimas gracias, tío.
Sr. Cárdenas:	De nada. Pero Diego, ¿puedes hacerme un favor? El Club Rotario está invitando a los estudiantes de intercambio a su reunión del día nueve. ¿Sería posible que vinieran tú y John?
Diego:	Sí, con mucho gusto.
Sr. Cárdenas:	Muy bien. Hasta el nueve. Adiós, Diego.

How is Diego going to pay his parking fine?

A. Diego will bribe the policeman. (Turn to p. 85, A)

B. His uncle will pay it for Diego. (Turn to p. 66, B)

C. Diego will not pay it because his uncle can get it fixed. (Turn to p. 90, C)

D. Diego can take it or mail it to the traffic court. (Turn to p. 109, D)

---

chasco disappointment, trick	**tránsito** traffic (court)	**letrero** sign
mordida bribe, payoff	**multa** fine	

48. ¿Dónde está el baño?

Inscribiéndose ° en un hotel, Madrid, España

Mr. Jones:	Tengo reservaciones para dos habitaciones. Somos cuatro.
Recepcionista:	Sí, señor. ¿Con pensión completa? °
Mr. Jones:	¿Qué comidas incluye?
Recepcionista:	El desayuno, señor.
Mr. Jones:	No, no queremos la pensión completa.
Recepcionista:	Bien. Hay dos cuartos en el séptimo piso. Botones, ° 786 y 788 por favor.
Botones:	Sí. Favor de pasar por aquí, señor.

(Más tarde en el cuarto)

Tommy:	Papá, ¿dónde está el baño?
Mr. Jones:	Ésa debe ser la puerta allá.
Tommy:	No, papá, es el armario.°
Mr. Jones:	Hmmm. Botones, ¿dónde está el baño?
Botones:	Al fin del corredor. Está cerca de este cuarto.
Mr. Jones:	¿En el pasillo? ° ¿No lo hay en este cuarto?
Botones:	No, señor, esta habitación es sin baño. Pero está cerca. Éste es un cuarto bueno.
Mr. Jones:	¿Ningún baño? ¡Caramba! ¿Qué clase de hotel es éste? El guía dice que es un buen hotel y, ¡no hay baño! ¡Qué chasco! Y además, tenemos cuartos reservados. ¡Por Dios! Mejor que solamente pasemos tres días en Madrid.

What misunderstanding has occurred to make Mr. Jones angry about the room?

A. The family had reservations and one should expect better rooms when reservations are made. (Turn to p. 108, A)
B. The family forgot to tip the bellboy and so he gave them poor rooms. (Turn to p. 76, B)
C. Mr. Jones indicated that he did not want a room with bath when he checked in. (Turn to p. 64, C)
D. If the family had taken breakfast with the room, they would have received better rooms. (Turn to p. 91, D)

---

inscribiéndose registering	**botones** bellboy	**armario** closet
pensión completa complete lodging		**pasillo** corridor

49. El piso perdido

Un hispanoamericano de Chicago está inscribiéndose en un hotel, Sevilla, España.

Sr. García:	Dos habitaciones, por favor.
Recepcionista:	Sí, señor. ¿Cuántos son ustedes?
Sr. García:	Somos cinco. Yo, mi esposa y tres hijos.
Recepcionista:	Tengo dos cuartos en el segundo piso, pensión completa.
Sr. García:	Muy bien. ¿Dónde firmo?°
Recepcionista:	Aquí, señor. Botones, 215 y 217.

(Más tarde en su cuarto)

Miguelito:	Papá, estamos en el tercer piso. ¿No dijo el recepcionista que estaríamos en el segundo?
Sr. García:	Sí, Miguelito. Es que el primer piso tiene techo° alto. Estamos en el segundo piso. Los cuartos son 215 y 217.
Miguelito:	No, papá. Ven acá. Mira.
Sr. García:	Miguelito, estoy ocupado. No importa. Si el recepcionista dice que es el segundo piso, entonces es el segundo piso.
Miguelito:	Mamá, ven acá. Estamos en el tercer piso.

Why does Miguelito keep insisting that they are on the third floor?

A. Miguelito is too young to count correctly. (Turn to p. 89, A)
B. Miguelito is right but they count differently in Spain. (Turn to p. 78, B)
C. Miguelito is a very stubborn child and will not admit that it is the second floor. (Turn to p. 97, C)
D. Sevilla is in the mountains and their room is at the back of the hotel. Because the hotel is on a hill, it seems as though their room is on the third floor at this side. (Turn to p. 63, D)

---

firmo I sign

techo ceiling

50. La muerte

Quito, Ecuador

Catalina: ¿Has oído que acaba de morir la abuela de Rosa?
Laurie: ¡Qué lástima!
Catalina: Aquí viene. Rosa, mi más sentido pésame.°
Rosa: Gracias, Catalina. Estamos tristes, tristísimas.
Laurie: Bueno, era vieja y estaba sufriendo. Está mejor ahora .
Por supuesto que la echarán de menos,° pero hay que
vivir. No hay mal que por bien no venga.
Rosa: No entiendes. Me voy. Hasta luego, Catalina.
Catalina: Voy al velorio ° esta noche. Hasta entonces.
(Rosa sale.)
Catalina: Ay, Laurie, ¿por qué dices eso? La abuela acaba de
morir. No entiendes lo mucho que todos la queríamos.
Es una tragedia.

What did Laurie do wrong?

A. Laurie should not have said anything because she does not
know Rosa well enough. (Turn to p. 104, A)
B. Laurie tried to see the good side of it which offended the Latin
Americans girls. (Turn to p. 87, B)
C. Laurie forgot to say *mi más sentido pésame,* which is always
the correct thing to say first. (Turn to p. 88, C)
D. Laurie should not speak of the grandmother's suffering so soon
after her death. (Turn to p. 70, D)

---

pésame condolence   **echarán de menos** you will miss   **velorio** wake

51. Voy a votar

Ponce, Puerto Rico

Connie: A mí me gusta mucho la política.
Yolanda: Tienes razón. Es muy interesante, especialmente ahora con las elecciones de este año.
Connie: Creo que los dos candidatos para presidente tienen sus ventajas.° Me gustan las ideas de uno y el otro es, personalmente, un hombre formidable.
Yolanda: Nosotros votamos por nuestros representantes. Lo que representan son las varias ideas para el futuro de Puerto Rico, sea independiente, sea estado de los Estados Unidos, o sea el Estado Libre Asociado que tenemos ahora. Yo francamente prefiero que Puerto Rico sea estado, aunque a mi papá le gusta el Estado Libre Asociado.
Connie: Claro que yo no tengo opinión en este asunto. Pero, ¿qué opinan los candidatos presidenciales?
Yolanda: No se meten en° los asuntos de Puerto Rico, y creo que no saben mucho de nuestros problemas. Por eso, no sé lo que opinan.
Connie: Bueno, aunque básicamente soy independiente, si las elecciones fueran mañana, votaría por el republicano para gobernador de mi estado, pero probablemente votaría por el demócrata para presidente. ¿Por quién piensas votar tú?
Yolanda: No voto en esa elección.
Connie: ¿No tienes dieciocho años?
Yolanda: Sí, los cumplí el mes pasado, y por eso voy a votar en las elecciones de Puerto Rico.
Connie: ¿No te interesa la campaña presidencial?
Yolanda: Claro me interesa. A todo el mundo le interesa.
Connie: Entonces, ¿por qué no vas a votar?
Yolanda: Sí, voy a votar, pero para presidente no puedo.

Why isn't Yolanda going to vote in the presidential election?

A. Although Yolanda is a citizen of the U. S., as a Puerto Rican she cannot vote for president. (Turn to p. 60, A)
B. Yolanda has not registered yet. (Turn to p. 73, B)
C. Since they are not interested in Puerto Rico, Yolanda does not see any sense in wasting her vote. (Turn to p. 58, C)
D. Puerto Ricans are not citizens of the U. S. (Turn to p. 89, D)

---

ventajas advantages   **no se meten en** they don't get involved in

52. Una manifestación

Mendoza, Argentina

Joe: Marcos, mira esta foto en el periódico. ¿No es éste el amigo de tu hermano mayor?

Marcos: ¿Cuál? Ah, sí. Es Alejandro Guzmán. Déjame leer este artículo, por favor.

Joe: Es de la manifestación de anoche. Aquí lo tienes.

Marcos: Dice que Alejandro es uno de los estudiantes activos en el movimiento para mejoramiento social. Yo sabía que le interesaba mucho la política, pero no me di cuenta de que era uno de los líderes.

Joe: ¿Es parte del grupo que participó en la manifestación?

Marcos: Sí. Joe, ¿por qué no vamos al centro esta noche? Sin duda, habrá otra manifestación. Podemos ir con mi hermano.

Joe: ¿Por qué te metes en eso?

Marcos: Los obreros automovilísticos están de huelga° y nosotros los estudiantes estamos en favor de la causa.

Joe: Tú estudias para médico, ¿verdad?

Marcos: Claro. Pero esta causa es muy importante para el país.

Joe: ¿Por qué hay una manifestación de estudiantes? Ustedes no están de huelga.

Marcos: Ahora no, pero si el gobierno no hace nada, tenemos que hacer algo.

Joe: Eso puede ser peligroso.

Marcos: Posiblemente, pero somos estudiantes y tenemos la seguridad de la universidad.

Why does Marcos want to get involved in the auto workers' strike?

A. His father works there. (Turn to p. 87, A)
B. Marcos wants to help his friend. (Turn to p. 81, B)
C. Many students are very active in politics and in causes such as this. (Turn to p. 70, C)
D. As a medical student, Marcos may be able to help if there is trouble. (Turn to p. 100, D)

---

están de huelga are on strike

53. El golpe de estado

La Paz, Bolivia

Sra. Ramos: Alfredo, ¿has oído las noticias esta mañana? Dice que hubo un golpe de estado° anoche.

Sr. Ramos: Y, ¿quién es el nuevo presidente? Hinojosa Silva?

Sra. Ramos: Sí, claro. Se ha efectuado.° Están en control. La cosa es que no sé si debo ir al hospital hoy o no. Siempre ayudo allí los miércoles.

Sr. Ramos: El hospital no está en el centro y si Jorge maneja, probablemente no haya peligro. ¿A qué hora vas?

Sra. Ramos: A las tres.

Sr. Ramos: Entonces, yo voy a mi oficina y te llamo más tarde para avisarte.° Mejor, regreso a casa hoy para la comida. Iba a almorzar con el Sr. Taylor de la Embajada de los Estados Unidos, pero con este golpe, estará ocupado hoy. Así te veo a la una.

Sra. Ramos: Ten cuidado, Alfredo.

Jorge: ¡Mamá! ¡Papá! ¡El Partido Nacional Revolucionario está en el poder! ¡Hubo golpe!

Sr. Ramos: Sí, ya sé. Por eso, Jorge, quiero que lleves a tu mamá al hospital si está bastante calma la ciudad.

Gary: ¿Vamos a salir de casa?

Jorge: ¡Ay, papaaaá! Quiero ir al centro.

Gary: ¡Al centro!

Jorge: Sí, tal vez habrá una celebración de parte del nuevo gobierno.

Sr. Ramos: Vamos a ver. Pero será mejor observar unas precauciones. Por eso, lleva a tu mamá al hospital.

Jorge: Bien, papá, pero, ¿puedo ir al centro esta noche?

Gary: ¿Durante una revolución?

Sr. Ramos: Les aviso a mediodía. Ahora me marcho.

Why is the family so calm if there is a revolution?

A. This is a common way for the government to change and often does not upset everyday citizens. (Turn to p. 69, A)
B. Sr. Ramos is an important official and would not be affected. (Turn to p. 90, B)
C. It is not a real revolution. That is just an expression for the new President. (Turn to p. 91, C)
D. They are just trying to act normal so as not to frighten Gary. (Turn to p. 102, D)

---

golpe de estado government takeover   **avisarte** to let you know
se ha efectuado carried out

Follow-ups

A. Correct. Carol obviously seems to understand the custom of the *paseo*, but the phrase *ocho días* confused her because she knows that the *paseo* will be next Sunday night. What Carol does not know is that the phrase *ocho días* means «in a week» in Spanish. Start with *today* and count the days until a week from now and you will see why. Can you guess what *quince días* means? Remember, every language has idioms that have a slightly different meaning from what the words literally say.

B. True! It would certainly be costly here in the United States to go to two movies, but in Mexico and many Spanish-speaking countries, the movies are very inexpensive. Since few people have television, most go to the movies and the large attendance helps keep the prices down. As soon as Jim realized that it would not be expensive, he agreed to go. When you travel to Mexico, go to the movies. It will not cost much and, even if you do not understand everything, it is a good way to learn Spanish faster.

C. This is the correct answer. Books, especially paperback books, often are sold with some or all of the pages uncut. This may bother North Americans who buy them if they think that they have an imperfect book for which they have paid full price. To the Spaniard or the Latin American, it simply means that it is indeed a new book, not a used one. It helps Americans in other countries to understand *why* different things are tolerated because there may be, as in the case of an uncut book, very good reasons for looking at things a different way.

D. If Beth is a typical North American girl, she probably does think she is overweight. But from what everyone is saying, it does not seem as though they think she is overweight. Gloria says she is thin and Pablo calls her *Flaquita* or «Skinny.» Does this clue help you to choose the correct answer?

A. Vicente is the first one to mention what a good cook his mother is. While it is true that maids often help them, the women of the house have charge of the kitchen and are proud to be good cooks. This would not be the reason that Vicente is angry. Try to find a better answer.

B. Right! The *paseo* is a favorite custom of the young people in Mexico, especially in the provincial cities and in the rural towns. Every Sunday night all the young people go to the town square. Actually, everybody in town goes. While the custom is changing, traditionally the boys walk clockwise and the girls walk counterclockwise around the square. It is a good chance to get to know each other. When the boys pick out a girl they like, they turn around and walk with her. Of course, her girlfriends are near and so are the children who play in the center near the bandstand, and also the adults who sit on the benches around the outside of the square. Everything is quite proper. There are ice cream and balloon vendors, a band concert and, quite often, decorations around the square. The *paseo* is a custom that the young people enjoy very much.

C. Actually, if the *voter* is informed, the vote is not wasted. But even if Yolanda thought that the presidential candidates were interested in Puerto Rico, she would still not vote for president. Try again to find the reason why.

D. Latin Americans have dances quite often and every time they do, they last as long as possible. Does this give you a clue as to the correct answer?

A. Correct! *Compadre* or *comadre* generally indicates the formal relationship between the parents of a child and the godparents of that child. That is the very special relationship that exists between Gregorio's mother and the chef of the Zaragozana Restaurant. Sometimes these terms are also used for very, very close and special friends. This may be the case with Julián and Gregorio, or since Julián is Eduardo's older brother, he may have a child and Gregorio may be the godfather of Julián's child.

B. Absolutely right! Work such as this (working on cars, working in the yard, making small home repairs) is not done by Latin Americans of the middle and upper classes, that is, by those who have the money to buy cars. That is considered work for a poor man who *has* to do such menial jobs. Latin Americans are not «do-it-yourself» advocates as we are in the U. S. Besides, that would be taking a job away from someone who really needs the job.

C. Absolutely correct! Independence Day in Paraguay is on May 14th. If you are ever in another country on an American holiday, you will probably feel quite homesick on that day because it is just another day to people in other countries (as May 14th is to us). However, there will be some pleasant surprises on other days on which we would not expect to have a holiday. Christmas and Easter are really the only two major holidays of ours that are celebrated in all the Spanish-speaking countries, but even then they do not necessarily celebrate the same way or on the same day we do.

D. His friend may be studying to become a priest, but Jesús is not used as a term of address for a priest. Try again.

A. You are absolutely right! Puerto Ricans are citizens of the United States, but as residents of a Commonwealth they cannot vote for president and vice-president. Although they do vote for senators and representatives, their congressmen do not have an official vote in the Congress. However, Puerto Ricans do not pay federal income tax either. Thus, while many Puerto Ricans desire statehood, there are many others who prefer their current commonwealth status. Still others, of course, prefer complete independence.

B. This is the correct answer from a North American's point of view. Amy played tennis in the sun too long and has a headache from it and sore muscles from playing so long when she seems to be out of condition. However, as far as cultural differences are concerned, North Americans are known for having back problems as a typical complaint and Latin Americans more customarily complain about liver problems. Do not be surprised if, in similar circumstances, a Latin American like Margarita complains of being bothered by her liver. They learn this as a part of their culture and do not consider it any more strange than we do a backache. This does not mean the aches and pains are not real, just that we learn to be sensitive to different things.

C. Correct! Fifty percent of the people of Peru are Indians. A large percentage of them do not speak Spanish but rather Quechua, the language the Incas spoke when the Spaniards arrived. In Mexico, Guatemala, Colombia, Ecuador and Bolivia, there are also large numbers of Indians who do not speak Spanish. This presents a number of problems for these countries.

D. This might be true but the conversation indicates that Jim is only going to take Carmen the following night. Try again.

A. This statement is true, although there is a better answer for this situation. Many, many Latin Americans enjoy literature. An American traveling in Latin America would notice the many bookstores and the quality of the books they sell. However, Tomás specifically says that he does not want to hear about school. He is thinking of something else. Can you find the correct answer with this hint?

B. While it is true that guests certainly would not be expected to help do such jobs as Janie is suggesting, they could help with some jobs, such as arranging flowers. This is a difficult question and this answer was about 90% correct. Try once more.

C. Absolutely correct! Sandy does not understand that, although both systems work the same way, the basic unit of a peso does not have to equal the basic value of a dollar. (Actually, the value of our own dollar changes right within our own country, so its basic value is not always the same.) While each country (such as Mexico, France, Germany, etc.) has a basic unit of money, with 100 subunits of it and with multiples of five, ten, etc., the relationship between the money of various countries varies. Each country has its own base value for its own basic unit of money. Emilia expressed this idea very well when she said, «Our money is *Mexican* money.» It does not have to be equal in value to another country's money.

D. Right! María has said nothing that is wrong for a Latin American girl. In the U. S., saying «God» in a situation such as this is not only impolite, but is considered swearing because it shows a lack of respect towards our view of religion. In Latin America it is not considered swearing. People find nothing wrong in asking God to help them in everyday situations. All three expressions, *Dios mío*, *Por Dios* and *Dios me ayude* are commonly used. An equivalent in English might be *Oh, heavens!* or *Oh, my goodness!*

A. Right! Different countries have different beauty standards. The fashionably thin American is too thin in Latin America. The men prefer the women to weigh a little more. (Maybe it is a way to tell who is a good cook.) The American girl who is 10-20 pounds over what she considers her ideal weight, is probably just right in Latin America.

B. Correct! In some parts of Latin America, especially Puerto Rico and Mexico, the words *tu madre* show a lack of respect for one's mother and therefore these words are not used unless one is provoking a fight. Even though they are used in a perfectly harmless situation such as in this conversation, the reaction is often instinctive. Phil should be saying, *tu mamá* instead of *tu madre*. Different words and phrases must be avoided in different countries. The Biblical·word «ass,» for example, must be used with some caution in this country. Learn to avoid the language «taboos» of other countries.

C. Mateo's parents are probably at the dance. Many dances in Latin America are held, not by schools, but by clubs (such as sports clubs and social clubs) and are for the entire family. Mateo's parents probably will dance the *cueca* also. However, they are probably already aware that Mateo can dance the *cueca*, so try again to find a better answer.

D. Correct. Cattle is extremely important to the economy of Argentina and many wealthy ranchers and their families will be at the show. An *exposición* such as this would be a social event and as Isabel says, movie and TV stars would be there. This reason, plus the fact that Latin Americans in general tend to dress up more than North Americans do, is why Isabel wants Marcia to dress up. Because Marcia is not aware of these cultural factors, she does not want to get dressed up as she should in this case. If you travel to Latin America, remember to take some clothes so you can dress up for special occaşions.

A. It is true, of course, that it is not his book, but Gerardo certainly does not seem to be that impolite in the conversation. There must be another reason for him not getting upset about the book. Try again.

B. Actually, a boyfriend in Latin America has to be a friend of practically all of the girlfriends of his girlfriend. The girls certainly do talk about the boys and to do this, they certainly have to admit knowing them. Try again to find the most probable reason.

C. While it is true that many Latin American men are smaller than average North American men, unless they were sick they would certainly have enough strength to change a tire. Remember that women change tires also in the U. S. Strength is not proportionate to height. Try to find a better answer.

D. Sevilla is not in the mountains although there are mountains in the distance. Sevilla is located on the Guadalquivir River and the city itself is on land that is quite flat. Look for another reason that Miguelito thinks they are on the third floor.

A. *Paseo* does not mean concert. *Paseo* means a walk and *concierto* means concert. Carol's problem here is not a misunderstanding about the language but rather a custom. Try again using this hint.

B. Saleswomen usually try to be nice and to be complimentary. This is normal behavior, but it is not the reason that she is so happy this time. Try again.

C. Correct! Although he did not realize it when Mr. Jones indicated that he did not want the room *con pensión completa,* the desk clerk understood it to mean without bath. Many European hotels have rooms without a bath because Europeans are accustomed to using a common bath that is located in each corridor. *Con pensión completa* means «with a bath,» and Americans who desire a room American-style must indicate this in making reservations and in checking into the hotel.

D. In some places, the girls cannot go out with a boy (even chaperoned) unless they have been formally introduced by a suitable mutual acquaintance, but they can and do know each other. After all, they have to make arrangements to be introduced! Can you think of another reason why Mela does not know who this boy is?

A. While it is true that in many parts of Latin America the traveler must be careful that the ice cubes are made from purified water, in the home the people are very careful to use water that is safe. A visitor to a home or an exchange student normally does not have to worry about this. Try again.

B. Absolutely correct! One of the effects of the *siesta* is that many stores and businesses close for about two hours in the middle of the day. If you have something important to buy, be sure to buy it early in the day. Some countries are trying to change this custom, but it usually takes a government order to do it. Most Spanish-speaking people consider the *siesta* an important part of their day. The long lunch hour gives them a chance to go home for lunch; and in some countries, it means not having to work during the hottest part of the day.

C. The remarks themselves certainly are not rude. They actually seem very complimentary. Try again.

D. Right! Latin Americans of the middle and upper classes have maids to do the housework. It is her job to do these things and Janie actually might be offending the maid by doing her work and thus suggesting that the maid is not doing it well. In spite of the strong habit to do such things as make the bed and to ask if one can help, an American should resist these impulses in Latin America. You will not be considered lazy. Notice what Mamá says in the conversation. She obviously does not understand Janie's intent in offering to help, because her suggestion is that they go to the movies.

A. Absolutely correct! In Spanish-speaking countries many people use both their father's family name and their mother's family name. Nevertheless, if only one name is used, it is the father's name. Luis's father's last name is Pérez and his mother's last name is Villarreal. If Nancy had referred to him as Luis Pérez, Mela probably would have identified him. The use of the wrong last name causes problems that are more serious than this. Puerto Rican students who move to New York City, for example, have a problem enrolling. The school official puts their last *apellido* on the records, not realizing that this is their mother's last name. To the Puerto Rican, this would indicate that the mother was not married to the father. The students and their mothers unfairly suffer dishonor from this cultural difference. English-speaking Americans should be very careful in learning names from other cultures. A «last» name may not be last.

B. No, his uncle will not have to pay it for him because there is another way to settle it. Look for another answer.

C. There *is* a difference between *adiós* and *hasta luego* but this is not it. *Hasta luego* (or a similar expression) is used when parting is fairly temporary and you will see each other soon. *Adiós* means that you do not expect to see the other person for a while; so *adiós* is used when one is leaving on a trip, for example. Nevertheless, one often hears, *Adiós, hasta luego* used together for both situations. Try again.

D. Alonso suggested that they go to the bank, which is the proper place to go to cash a check. Try again.

A. Bolivia does not have a holiday the first week in July. Although flowers are given for special events, they are also often given for no special reason. Does this give you a clue to help you find a better answer?

B. The *paseo* is held every Sunday and she does say that she is especially enjoying herself this week in particular. Probably she just likes being with Miguel. Try again to find why she is confused about when the *paseo* is held.

C. The first part of this answer is obviously true. While the cost of living is very high in Puerto Rico and the average income is low by mainland standards, nevertheless, Puerto Rico ranks above the rest of Latin America. There is a sizeable and growing middle class in Puerto Rico and there are also some very wealthy Puerto Ricans. However, Julio is surely not thinking about Puerto Rico in general at this time. His concern is more personal. Using this as a hint, try to find the best answer for this situation.

D. Correct! *Gazpacho* is supposed to be served cold. It is a little like tomato juice served in a soup bowl. Sally is not accustomed to having soups served cold, although some restaurants here do serve consommé which is chilled also. If you order something in another country and it is not served as you expected, ask if it really is supposed to be served that way (waiters in other countries occasionally make mistakes too), and if it is, try it; you might like it. Besides, you will have the adventure of eating foods that are different so when people talk about them, you will at least know what they are talking about.

A. ·You are correct! This conversation is an example of Latin American *machismo* meeting with North American «Women's Lib» and it is going to cause some conflicts in Latin America. One of the ways *machismo* is demonstrated is by protecting and providing for women who are considered weaker. Julio's pride in being manly would suffer if he allowed a woman to pay in these circumstances. *Machismo* is very important to Latin American men and to allow someone to show that they are not *muy macho* would be a loss of honor and prestige in the community.

B. *Compadre* is not another word for cousin. Besides, Julián would not be introducing his brother, Eduardo, to his own cousin. Try again.

C. Latin Americans in general dress up more than North Americans do, especially when going out with a date. Nevertheless, to the extent that pants are in style and are suitably dressy, the girls would wear pants on a date. Try again.

D. A Latin American is proud of his country and would certainly not object to a North American taking pictures unless, of course, the American is rude, intrudes into a private place, always focuses on poverty, or is in a restricted area (like their version of Fort Knox). The subject matter of the pictures that Rich is taking is not the reason for Carlos' and Mario's concern. Try again to find the real reason that they do not want any more pictures taken.

A. This is the most probable answer. The *golpe de estado,* or unconstitutional takeover of the government, is the most common cause of change in government. Most of them are changes in personnel only, and as Sr. Ramos says, do not actually change the government much as far as most citizens are concerned. Of course, government officials would be affected and also people very active in a political party. Sometimes there is some fighting for a few days when armed resistance occurs but rarely a full scale revolution occurs. In this case, the radio reports seem to indicate that the new government is in control already. The *golpe de estado* is not limited to Bolivia. Other governments in Latin America also change in this manner.

B. Although the value of the basic unit may be different, the numerical system is the same. Both Mexican pesos and American dollars use the metric system or a base ten concept. Just as both apples and oranges are types (different from each other, of course) of fruit, both pesos and dollars are real money.

C. In Latin America it is true that cooking, except professionally, is almost always a woman's role. However, Phil is an Ohioan and has explained that it is his hobby, as it is for many American men. This is part of our culture and it is certainly not wrong for Phil to admit it. There is a better answer.

D. Latin American men of the middle and upper classes are almost always very nicely dressed, but this would not prevent them from getting their clothes dirty in an emergency. However, this is not an emergency and is not the reason that Nacho is impressed. Try again.

A. It does take much time and patience to learn another language and Patty did make a mistake here. Under the circumstances, we who speak English can understand why she made the mistake. When you find the correct answer, you will understand her mistake.

B. Correct! Spanish-speaking people rarely use saints' names or names that are used for human beings to name animals. They do not consider animals «almost human» as we sometimes do. Animals are not pets but rather have a purpose, such as a watchdog. Other names for dogs besides those in the conversation are: *Terror, Pinto, Yaqui, Cazán* and the American-inspired names of *Dogo, Dogui* and *Mannix.* Some common names for cats are: *Blanquita, Cenicienta, Minina, Perla Pinta, Bonbon, Jazmín* and *Pelusa.*

C. Correct! Much more so than in the U. S., both high school and university students are active in politics and social struggles. Students often play a major role in bringing down a government. Universities are autonomous; that is, they are not controlled by the government. Thus, causes can be developed and strengthened at the university, and the students (with some recent exceptions) have the protection and security of being on the campus onto which the government forces cannot intrude. Thus, one of the first actions of a revolutionary government in Latin America is to close the universities and sometimes some high schools as well.

D. It would have been better if she had mentioned the suffering and stopped there. Try to find another answer.

A. This is a true statement, but it is not the reason she does not want to get dressed up to go to a cattle show. She would not be riding a horse anyway. Try again.

B. Right! Jesús was Christ's given name, and the name Jesús is still used often in Latin America. Other names that are used in this category are Angel and Trinidad for boys, and Concepción, Encarnación and Rosario for girls. Religious symbols are more evident in everyday life in Latin America, even in names. Another example of a religious name is the country, El Salvador.

C. Carlos and his friends may be experts at football because many Latin Americans play this game extremely well, but this is not the reason in this case. Carlos has stated that he and his friends are *not* experts and has continued to ask Tom to join them. Try again.

D. This is the correct answer. When passing on the street without stopping to talk, one says *adiós*. This originated from the religious sense of «Go with God.» Patty thought that the two women were saying the literal equivalent of hello, which we say in English in this situation. When she tried to say hello by using *adiós*, she made a mistake since it is not used in that situation. Spanish-speaking people say the literal equivalent of goodbye when they pass like this on the street, instead of hello. Older people seem to say this more often, perhaps simply because the younger people always seem to stop and talk.

A. You are right! Taking many pictures is an activity that interests Americans much more than Latin Americans. Therefore, Latin Americans often cannot understand why Americans want to take so many pictures. They sometimes become impatient with the American photographer. They take pictures, of course, but many fewer than we do. They may get everyone together for one picture to remember the day, then put the camera away so that it does not interfere with other activities. Also, do you remember seeing cartoons of Americans abroad—loaded down with cameras and equipment? Now you can probably give one reason why Americans are easy to identify when on vacation.

B. Cheryl is an American who probably thinks women should have some rights. But this does not necessarily mean that she does not like boys who are *macho*. Actually, if you read carefully, what she objects to is almost the opposite. Try again.

C. Correct! Many Mexican girls have the name María and although we do not think of this as a boy's name (how about Chris, Pat or Kim?), it is a very common second name for boys in Mexico. Did you know that there are several girls' names that end in –o? Amparo, Consuelo and Rosario are examples. María is the only «girl's» name that is commonly used for boys and it is used because of its religious meaning. José María is a very common combination. One of Mexico's great heroes was José María Morelos and one of Cuba's great poets was José María Heredia.

D. This is the correct answer. In many of the Latin American countries, the government does not recognize the religious ceremony and the church does not recognize a civil ceremony. Therefore, many couples do have two ceremonies. For most, the civil ceremony is just a formality, similar to getting a license, although they are legally married as far as the government is concerned. The religious ceremony is the important one for the family and the one after which all the festivities occur. The family and friends do not consider the couple married until after the ceremony in church.

A. This is correct. In Europe and in many parts of Latin America, it is the custom to tip the ushers for their service, just as you would tip a waiter or a bellhop. Before going to a theater, a movie or a concert, check to see if you should expect to give a tip and how much would be expected.

B. Of course, this is possible, but Yolanda does say that she intends to vote in the Puerto Rican elections, so she will eventually have to register. Look for a better reason that she is not going to vote for president.

C. Correct! In many Spanish-speaking countries, boys use the traditional *abrazo* or embrace when they meet. They also walk down the street, one with an arm over the other's shoulders. They are *compañeros* or buddies and it is perfectly correct for them to put arms around each other. Cheryl is not used to this because American boys, although they may be very good friends, do not have much personal physical contact. Girls in Spanish-speaking countries also walk arm-in-arm or hold hands on the street. It is common to do so and no one thinks anything of it.

D. Yes, this is correct. Bob has not yet accepted the *mañana* philosophy. Getting things done «on time» is a North American concept which is not widely accepted among Spanish-speaking people. Other characteristics of this informal attitude towards time are: 1) not getting things done very rapidly; 2) arriving late for appointments; and 3) spending more time at the table at mealtime than we do, etc. Americans often are very frustrated by this and imply that Latin Americans are «lazy.» This is not true, of course, but is a result of the different viewpoint of time.

A. 100% correct! Here in the United States saying the equivalent of *negrita* would be an insult. In Latin America, there is little discrimination on the basis of skin color. Many Latin Americans themselves are of a mixed racial background. Besides, the ending *–ita* is one that shows endearment or liking. *Pablo* becomes *Pablito, mamá* becomes *mamacita,* and *chica* becomes *chiquita.* Although the American girls feel they have been insulted, the young man was actually complimenting them. This kind of a compliment, said to a woman in passing on the street, is called a *piropo* and is a common custom. What is an insult in one country may be a compliment in another.

B. This is true, but most North Americans do not expect everything to be absolutely perfect either. However, different people tolerate different imperfections and errors for different reasons. Look for a more specific reason that Gerardo is not concerned about Ron's book.

C. Absolutely correct. Many young men recite poetry to their girlfriends in Latin America. Both of them consider it very romantic and, of course, it also shows that he is intelligent. Until recent years (and even now in small towns) there was always a chaperone present with an unmarried couple and reciting poetry was also a way to communicate ideas without upsetting the chaperone. The custom of chaperoning has partly changed; the custom of reciting poetry to a girl hasn't.

D. Pedro may have been sick but nothing in this conversation indicates that. Felipe is not treating him like an invalid. There is another reason for the way he is acting and that is what Cheryl is upset about. Using this clue, try again.

A. It is true that saying Jesús is not considered swearing in Latin America. But this is not the reason that Beto keeps saying this in the conversation. Try again.

B. Josefina says there is a ceremony today and also that she and Antonio are going to be witnesses. It seems as though they are doing more today than just getting a license. Go back and try to find a better answer.

C. Sometimes this is true and sometimes it is not. At times a North American with money gets a great deal of attention in tourist areas. This can cause resentment by the Latin Americans and may be one reason why Americans are not too well liked in some places. However, in this case that is not the reason that they are not giving him his turn. Try to find a better answer.

D. This is the most plausible answer. Many Latin Americans do not drink very cold drinks and seldom put ice in such drinks as lemonade, water or a soft drink. Cold drinks are thought to be harmful to the body, just as Margarita says. If your hosts in Latin America provide ice for your drinks, they may be acquainted with our «peculiar» habit of drinking iced drinks and perhaps they are being very thoughtful and polite. They put cold drinks in the same category as we put a cold draft of air. (Overheated homes are considered another North American peculiarity.) Urban Latin America uses ice more frequently.

A. Absolutely right! A drugstore in Latin America is not a de
    partment store, a supermarket, a stationery store or a jewelry
    store. Most stores in Latin America tend to be more limited
    in what is sold. A supermarket sells mainly food. A book-
    store sells books, not games and office supplies. When one
    goes shopping, it is customary to go to more stores than a
    shopper would here, since each shop has its own specialty.

B. They may have forgotten to tip the bellboy but he is not
    responsible for the rooms to which they have been assigned.
    He should be given a tip for showing where the rooms are and
    for carrying the luggage even if the rooms themselves are not
    satisfactory. Look again for a reason that Mr. Jones is angry.

C. *Gazpacho* certainly is a tomato soup, and as Jaime explained, it
    usually has certain vegetables added to it, such as green pep-
    pers, onions, cucumbers, etc. If Sally did not like tomato
    soup, she probably would not have ordered it in the first place.
    Try again.

D. Nothing the young man says in this conversation is disrespect-
    ful in Spanish. Americans who feel this way and who do not
    understand the language or the customs of another country will
    certainly find much to be angry about. You are about 90%
    correct in choosing this answer. But let's assume that Sandra
    and Doris are usually very friendly Americans. See if you can
    find another more specific reason for their anger.

A. Good! This is the correct answer. The young people of other countries, in addition to liking the modern dances such as the latest rock, also like to dance their national folk dances. In Chile and Argentina, they dance the *cueca;* in Venezuela, the *joropo;* and in Mexico, the *jarabe tapatío* (Mexican Hat Dance). Mateo wants to dance the *cueca* because it is a Chilean favorite, and it is a lively and fun dance. It is also quite easy to learn.

B. This might be partly true, but it is not the entire reason. Margarita would object to the ice water at any time, and even says in the conversation that Amy is always drinking too much cold water. Use this hint and try again to find the best answer.

C. Taking many pictures *is* slowing them down and they probably *do* have other things to do, but Latin Americans are often behind in schedule and would not be concerned by being detained a few minutes longer. There is another reason that Carlos and Mario want Rich to stop taking so many pictures. Go back and see if you can find it.

D. If Cristobal's godfather's name is also Cristobal, then they would celebrate on the same day. Does this give you a clue so that you can choose the right answer?

A. It is not customary to put the mother's first name on the letter. Juanita has the name correct, however. This is a difficult problem. Try again.

B. Miguelito is right and this answer is right. In Europe and many other parts of the world, they do count the floors of a hotel differently than we do in the United States. In Spain, the floor on which you enter is the ground floor, the floor above that is the first floor, and the floor above that the second floor, etc. The desk clerk who is Spanish is correct from his point of view in saying they will be on the second floor. Miguel is correct from an American point of view in insisting that they are on the third floor. Actually, Sr. García is also correct in saying that if the clerk said it was the second floor, it is the second floor. In Spain, which is where they are, it is the second floor. Remember that when you are in another country, it is helpful to use the standards and point of view of that country so things are not quite as confusing.

C. The band concert is part of the *paseo*. Carol should realize this because she is at a *paseo* during this conversation. The *paseo* and band concert are always Sunday evenings. Try to find another reason for her confusion.

D. This is true and is the correct answer. It is hard for us to consider a fish as a real pet. For Latin Americans, dogs, cats, birds, fish, etc. are all in the same category. They are mere animals, do not have human characteristics, and are not compared to humans. While Latin Americans have dogs for watchdogs and birds for their songs, they are not considered pets and would not usually be allowed in the house. There is not even a word for «pet» in Spanish.

A. All women have their own way of showing that they are angry or upset. María has done nothing inconsistent in showing her frustration with the situation. Does this clue help you to recognize the correct answer?

B. Latin Americans are polite under most circumstances but, in this case, he does not have to console Scott. Try again.

C. While dogs are often used as watchdogs and while some night watchmen may have dogs with them, this is not the reason that Maribel does not understand the American young peoples' actions. Try again.

D. This would be the correct answer from a Latin American's point of view. Just as North Americans are famous for their aching backs, typical Latin Americans are known for their liver problems. They have learned this as a part of their culture and do not consider it any more peculiar than we do our backaches. You probably know now what the correct response is for a North American, but you may consider this one a correct answer if you wish.

A. Felipe does not seem to be paying attention to either of the girls. In this part of Mexico, it is common for the boys to go to events (like rodeos, etc.) together and leave the girls at home. Try to find something else that is bothering Cheryl.

B. Nothing the young man says indicates that this is true. Besides, purse snatching, especially in the main plaza, is rare in Latin America. Actually he is complimenting them. Try again to find the reason that they are angry.

C. Only Julián and Gregorio are calling each other *compadre*, so it is not a word that can be used like *hombre* and *chico*. Besides, Eduardo says that Gregorio's mother is the *comadre* of the chef of the Zaragozana Restaurant which implies a more formal relationship. Look for another explanation of the words *compadre* and *comadre*.

D. Correct! In Spain and in many parts of Latin America, wine is the usual beverage that is served with meals. In some restaurants a pitcher of wine is included with the meal. There are no age requirements for drinking wine or any other kind of alcoholic beverage. Young people can and do drink at an earlier age than most American young people. Having wine with meals, however, is not even considered drinking in these countries, and very young children are often given a little wine with their meals. If you are from a French or an Italian family, you probably understand this custom very well.

A. While few Latin American teenagers have cars of their own to drive around in, age is not a factor in changing tires. There are certainly teenagers who have jobs changing tires in Latin America. Does this give you a clue as to the correct answer?

B. Actually it is his brother's friend. While Marcos may want to help Alejandro, there is a better reason for Marcos wanting to get involved in the strike. Try again.

C. Perhaps, but she does not have any of the other symptoms, such as a fever. Try to find another answer that could explain what is wrong with her.

D. Correct! Julie apparently has the Mexican *tortilla* in mind which is a flat, corn pancake-like item. In Spain, a *tortilla* is an omelet. The same word in Spanish may have different meanings in different countries.

A. Actually Mexican and Spanish soups are very much alike, except that Spanish soups are often made with olive oil. The word *picante* means hot in terms of spiciness and the word *caliente* means hot in terms of heat. Does this clue help you?

B. They *will* be late meeting the girls but being late is customary in Latin America. The girls really will not expect Carlos and Mario to be on time, so this is probably not the reason they do not want Rich to take any more pictures. Go back and see if you can find the real reason.

C. Absolutely correct! They are not late yet, so why should he worry? Latin Americans have a more informal view of time than we do, and are not compelled to do everything «on time» as most Americans are. For a party, they can arrive an hour «late» and still arrive earlier than most of the guests. If a party supposedly starts at 9:00, it will really get going about 11:00.

D. Latin American men, in general, are known for their *machismo* and this is often shown by being especially strong and agressive where a female is concerned. Nevertheless, after a half hour of dancing to rock music, no one would question it if he took Peggy for some refreshments. Actually, that is what Mateo intended to do until he heard the next dance. This clue should help you to go back and find the correct answer.

A. Maybe she was not good at math, but she is doing well in this conversation in the numerical difference between pesos and dollars. Does this clue help you to find the correct answer?

B. Right! While some things cost a great deal more money in Mexico than in the U. S. (cars, electric appliances and American cosmetics), most services and Mexican-made products are considerably less expensive. The problem is that even though an American may know that it costs less, they do not know the going rate. Although they pay less than they would at home and think it is a bargain, they pay more than a Mexican would. Naturally, the salespeople want to earn all they can from those they consider rich, but it also causes Mexicans and other Latin Americans to resent the North Americans because sometimes the Mexicans themselves eventually have to pay a higher price. This is one of the reasons that we sometimes seem to be «ugly» Americans.

C. Although this is not correct in this case, normally this is a true statement. The fashionably thin North American girl is not so much in fashion in Latin America. She looks undernourished to them. The North American girl who is 10 to 15 pounds overweight will be completely accepted in Latin America as having a great figure.

D. True! This is exactly what most North American girls think when Spanish men make these complimentary remarks which are called *piropos*. Chavela does not see anything unusual in what the young man is saying to them; but Lynn, who is not used to it, thinks that he is annoying them. She does not realize that when a young Spaniard sees a pretty girl, he is expected to make these remarks. The Spanish girls pretend to ignore them but really enjoy this custom, and are flattered by the attention.

A. Sometimes it is difficult for an American to understand everything that is said in another language. This answer may be true, but let's assume that Julie's Spanish is pretty good. There is another answer that is better.

B. Right! Latin Americans often celebrate their name day. Cristóbal's name day is *el Día de San Cristóbal*, July 24. He will celebrate then rather than his birthday which is the 11th. This day is referred to as his *día de santo*. The equivalent expression of our «Happy Birthday» for a name day is *Feliz Onomástico*.

C. Mexican girls also like to go in cars as often as they can, very much like American girls. They may not be able to do so as much and may have to walk more, but whether or not they like it is a personal opinion. In this case, Alicia does want to walk. There is another choice that better tells why they are not communicating.

D. Congratulations! This is the correct answer. Although Latin Americans have a game called *futbol,* it is what we refer to as soccer. Therefore when Tom arrived at the field and saw exactly how they were playing, he was correct in saying that he did not know how to play. Although few Americans play soccer, millions of Latin Americans do play this game. It is their most popular sport.

A. This would have been a correct answer except that when they returned to the car, the policeman or guard was not around. Contrary to the accepted custom in the U. S., giving a *mordida* or payoff to an official is common in Latin America. The policemen are not well–paid and appreciate the «gift,» and it is much less trouble to settle an infraction immediately and not have to go through red tape to settle it later. Of course, the policeman lectures the offender on the proper rules and cautions him or her not to do it again. While the answer you chose is accepted behavior in Latin America, it is not the answer to this question.

B. Pilar's father certainly may believe that young people should learn to handle drinking under the supervision of their parents, but in this situation, that belief would not make any difference. He would permit her to drink wine anyway. Try again.

C. While it is true that many North Americans do not bargain, it is because they do not know about it or because they do not know how, rather than because they have so much money. So while this answer may be partly true, it is not the correct *reason*. Try again.

D. Correct! It is the custom to have flowers decorate the house in Latin America and most families have fresh flowers in several rooms of the house. Flowers are inexpensive and many people buy them. There are flower markets in many cities and flowers stands in every market. For special occasions, even more flowers are used. When you travel to Latin America, you will find that many smaller hotels put fresh flowers in your room every day.

A. Where else in the city could they enjoy such a nice day? Buen Retiro is a large, beautiful park where everyone goes on a nice day. Anyway, there are other things to do in the park besides walk, such as rent boats. Try to find a better explanation of what is bothering her.

B. Yes, there is a 4th of July in Paraguay. It is right between the 3rd of July and the 5th of July. However, this answer was meant to trick you and you really are on the right track. Go back and figure out the correct answer now.

C. In Latin America and in Spain, the kind of talking the young man is doing in this conversation is a common custom called the *piropo*. This is a complimentary remark given to a woman passing on the street and will occur with all women. Try again.

D. Arriving late would not insult a Latin American. He would not even notice that it is late. Does this clue help you to find the correct answer?

A. His father may work there since, as in this country, the children of blue collar workers more and more often are going to the university. However, Joe and Marcos would have known about the situation if this were the case, instead of having to read about it in the newspaper. Try to find a better answer.

B. Right you are! North Americans sometimes try to be optimistic and cheer people up in order to help them overcome a tragedy, and Laurie was doing this. Latin Americans are pessimistic in such a situation. The others are the ones who say sad things, and then the bereaved person can have the satisfaction of rising above the tragedy. An American's best course of action is to say *mi más sentido pésame* and let the others carry on from there.

C. Latin Americans do think that all Americans are rich, but this is not the reason that Janie is not given the opportunity to help. She is not being given special treatment. Does this clue help you to choose the correct answer?

D. One dollar is currently worth about 145 pesos and one dollar will buy what 145 pesos will buy. One dollar will therefore obviously buy more than one peso. It also means that Americans have fewer dollars than Mexicans have pesos if they are equally well off. Saying that Americans have more money because a dollar is worth more is false logic. Look again.

A. It is wintertime in Paraguay in July and August, but July 4th is still July 4th. The seasons are reversed, not the calendar. By the way, the wintertime temperatures in Paraguay are in the 60's at night and the 70's in the daytime. Try again to find out what the problem is about the 4th of July.

B. This is probably true. Alfredo states that the man is an Indian, and many Indians who live in the *altiplano* near Cuzco come into Cuzco on market days. However, if this were the only reason, he could at least have said that he was not from Cuzco either. Look for another explanation.

C. It would have been better if she had said *mi más sentido pésame* which is always correct to say for a death, but it does not *have* to be said and does not necessarily have to be said first. Try again.

D. Some things, such as Mexican-made items, do cost less in Mexico; others cost more. The reason is not that the money is worth more or less, or whether they are paid for in dollars or in pesos. While this may add to Sandy's confusion, it is not the reason for her misunderstanding. Try again.

A. If Miguelito can talk this well, he can probably count to three. Look for another reason.

B. The *Exposición de Ganadería* is not like an American fair, although Marcia probably thinks it is. She asked about the rides and was told that there were not any. Being a North American, she would probably like to wear jeans anyway. This answer is partly correct; try to find the best answer.

C. Correct! At a market, it is the custom to bargain for the final price. Karen paid more than she should have because she accepted the first price given. She should have given a figure at about 1/2 to 2/3 of that first price. The final price would usually be about 60% to 80% of the first price mentioned.

D. Yes, Puerto Ricans are citizens of the United States. However, as citizens of a commonwealth, there are certain responsibilities and certain privileges that they do not have. Use this clue to go back and find the correct answer.

A. Luis Buñuel is probably the most outstanding Spanish film director. His pictures have won many awards and have been shown all over the world. While Jim may not be interested, there is a better reason for his not wanting to go. Try again.

B. If Sr. Ramos were an important official of the government or well known in politics, he would be one of the first to be affected. The fact that his wife told him that she had heard it on the radio indicates that, as far as the government is concerned, he is not important. Try again.

C. Correct. Getting a ticket fixed or otherwise helping a relative or close friend is accepted behavior in Latin America. It is called *amiguismo* and is a very strong custom. It might help one to get a job or to buy a bargain, but one of its most helpful features is to avoid red tape. Contrary to our North American belief, Latin Americans see nothing wrong in doing this kind of favor for each other.

D. This could be true but if Gerardo thought that there really were something wrong with the book and the bookstore owner were a friend of his father, it would be easy enough to exchange it. There is a concept called *amiguismo* in Latin America in which they save the best and do their best for a friend. Look for a better answer.

A. While it is true that, in a sense, the Guatemalan parents can select the day on which their children will celebrate, there is a very definite factor on what that day is based. Go back and see if you can discover it.

B. A traffic officer or an insurance salesperson might argue that this is the correct answer in any country, but let's assume that María is driving safely under rather annoying conditions. Try to find out what is wrong with *what* she is saying.

C. If by revolution you mean a war to change the basic political, social and economic structure, then it would not be a revolution. But if you mean a change of government apart from constitutional process (called a *golpe de estado*), then it would be a revolution. However, this is not the best answer in this situation. Try again.

D. The truth is that breakfast probably goes with the room anyway, even this one. It is the custom in Europe to serve a continental breakfast (hard rolls and coffee) with the price of the room. There must be another reason that Mr. Jones is upset. Try again.

A. If you think of our slums, you will realize that this is not true. It does seem as though North Americans vacationing or spending time in Mexico have a great deal of money. This may be what Luisa believes, but what would be the *reason* for it?

B. There may be more flowers in the house in the summertime, but July in Bolivia is wintertime because it is south of the equator. La Paz has plenty of flowers even in their wintertime because they are brought in from tropical valleys which are not far away. Try again.

C. Even those on a diet should eat some breakfast and it really does not seem like he has ordered that much. Try to find another explanation.

D. *Compadre* is not a slang term but rather a very formal term in Spanish with a specific meaning. Also, in the conversation Eduardo says that Gregorio's mother is a *comadre,* and he probably would not be using a slang term about her. Try again for the answer.

A. It is true he might want to talk to Carlota but, in this case, that is not the reason he is not worried about being late. Besides, most Latin Americans (men and women), contrary to many American men, really do like to go to parties. Can you find another explanation?

B. This might be true, of course, but she would probably be talking more in that case, asking where they are from, for example. There is another reason she is waiting in this case. See if you can find the reason.

C. It is true that girls and boys often go to different schools, but they definitely do get to know each other. They are especially likely to know their friends' friends. Look for another reason.

D. This could be true. U. S. money is accepted in a great many places around the world, but Luisa would not necessarily disapprove of that. Try to find the reason that she does not like what Karen is doing.

A. Playing football right after eating a big breakfast is not a very good idea in any country. In Chile, however, eating a continental breakfast is the custom. This usually consists of hard rolls and coffee. While this statement might be true in some cases, there is another more evident reason here. Try again.

B. Sometimes *gazpacho* needs to be chilled more but *not* warmed up. Does this clue help you to find the correct answer?

C. The conversation does not say that Margarita has some hot lemonade ready, although she would probably be happy to prepare some. This is a common remedy for a cold or headache. Try again.

D. This may be true but nothing in this conversation lets us know for sure. Americans should always be polite if possible in other countries. In this case, that is not what is causing the communications gap. Try again.

A. Of course the young Latin Americans (like the young North Americans) should have permission to stay out late, but this is not the reason that they are staying so late. Since dances usually include all ages in Latin America, it is quite probable that the adults are still there also.

B. This may be true but many people here also tell you only what you want to hear. Many of us hear only what we want. However, in this case, Bob is certainly not hearing what he wants to hear about his camera. Try again.

C. Josefina says that Mary Lou is correct in saying the wedding is a week from Sunday, so there is more than just the family celebration a week from Sunday. Go back and try to find a better answer.

D. Many Latin Americans do prefer North American products and Meche probably realizes the drugstore may very likely have some American products. And Mary Jo has said that it does not matter to her. Look for another reason.

A. The purse is inexpensive but probably not «cheap.» Most Mexicans are justly proud of the folk arts and folkcrafts such as this and often take them as gifts to people in the U. S. Look for another reason.

B. The crowd does seem to be making him nervous, but rather than the crowd itself, it is probably the way the crowd is acting to which he is not accustomed. Besides, he seems willing enough to get his check cashed and also the others do not seem to be paying attention to him. Try to find a better answer.

C. Young people of any age can drink wine. Very young children are often given a little wine with their meals. Try again.

D. Other countries, including Paraguay, certainly do celebrate political and national holidays. Because it is a different government, Independence Day in Paraguay is not celebrated on July 4th. This hint should help you to go back and find the correct answer.

A. In Spain and Latin America, it is very difficult to be late because they have a much more relaxed view about being on time than we do. Besides, it really would not take too long to buy just one thing. Try again.

B. While it does seem as though vacationing North Americans have a great deal of money, Luisa would certainly have enough to buy a purse if she wished. And while there are certainly some very poor Mexicans, Mexico has one of the highest average standards of living of the Latin American countries. Try again.

C. He does seem to be a very stubborn child because he keeps insisting that he is correct. However, the question really is why he is so stubborn about this. Look for the reason why he keeps insisting they are on the third floor.

D. Nothing in the conversation indicates that she knows Linda and nothing indicates that Linda has been ill, so we really do not know if this is true. Go back and find another reason why the saleswoman is happy.

A. Surprise! You are absolutely correct. The word *embarazada* is a false cognate. It does not mean embarrassed as an American might think, but is a widely used expression for being pregnant. Like most Latin Americans on hearing such news, the saleswoman is very happy about it. When Linda finds out what she has said, she will really be embarrassed. She should have said *Me da pena* or *Tengo vergüenza*.

B. Beth herself says she is fine, and that she is trying to lose weight, not to gain weight. She does not need a special diet; she is just not eating much in general. She is a typical North American girl. Try again.

C. The Císneros may be wealthy but this is not the reason that they have many flowers. Flowers are inexpensive in most Latin American countries. Does this clue help? Try again.

D. We hope Dave and Bill are gentlemen, since they are Americans in another country. But in this case, they do not have to walk her back up the aisle to be considered gentlemen. There is something else that they should do. Try again.

A. Yes, young people are permitted to drink Chilean wine, but they are also permitted to drink any other kind of wine from anywhere else. Since Chilean wine is excellent and, in general, less expensive than imported wines, many Chileans do prefer Chilean wine. Try again to find the answer to this question.

B. Correct! The dances usually do last until *las mañanitas*. Five in the morning would be a good guess as to when it will end. If you go to a dance in Latin America, get enough sleep the night before.

C. Of course María's mother might like her to be ladylike but in this situation, María's mother might very likely say the same thing. However a North American mother probably would not agree. Does this clue tell you which answer to choose?

D. Maybe she has forgotten what Alicia told her when Miguel invited her to go (See *El paseo*). But in this case, it is probably something else. Look for another reason for her confusion.

A. She does seem to have several things wrong with her in this conversation, but let's assume that she is not a hypochondriac. Besides, she probably would not have been selected as an exchange student if she was always complaining about something. Try again.

B. No one likes to admit that they have made a mistake. However, in this case, Juanita is correct. Do not admit that you chose this answer if you do not want to, but try another one.

C. Actually they forgot to do something else which would let her know that they no longer need her services. Does this clue help you to find the correct answer?

D. Marcos may be studying to be a doctor but he is still a student, and probably would not be able to help much in a crisis. Try to find a better reason.

A. Correct! For example, Latin Americans wait in line to buy a movie ticket, but they do not wait in line at a bank window. The cashier will take the check, give you a number, and then you wait until your number is called. If Jeff stands as though he were in a line, others think that he is waiting for his number to be called and step in ahead of him to give their requests to the cashier. What Jeff thinks is rude is actually the correct way of doing business there. Latin Americans think that we are rude under exactly the same circumstances. We make people stand in line while the one at the front monopolizes the time of the cashier who could, perhaps, be making more effective use of his time by taking care of more than one transaction at a time.

B. Tomás seems to be able to carry on a conversation quite well. Although he is talking about poetry in this conversation, let's assume that he can converse on other topics. Try to find a better answer.

C. Of course it is polite to offer guests something to eat, just as it is in the U. S. However, they have already offered her something to eat and they all want her to eat *more*. Try to find a reason for this.

D. If you went to the market in Cuzco, which is certainly a public place, you would hear the Indians talking a great deal. This is not the reason the Indian did not speak to the boys. Try again.

A. Many North American housewives are also perfectionists, but this is not the reason that Mamá does not expect Janie to help. Try again.

B. Cats, birds, dogs, turtles and fish are all in the same category as far as Latin Americans are concerned. Does this give you a clue as to why Maribel does not understand?

C. Marisol says that it is not a holiday. If it were, the stores would probably be closed all day long. Try again.

D. If they are just acting normal so as not to frighten Gary, and if it really is a dangerous revolution, they are overdoing it, don't you think? If it were a warfare–type revolution, Sra. Ramos would not continue with her normal schedule, and Sr. Ramos would not be going downtown to his office. They probably *are* acting normally in this situation, rather than just trying to act that way. Try again.

A. No, Anita and Fernando are the only ones who are going to be married according to this conversation. Try again.

B. This might be true but he is the one who suggested going for refreshments. Go back and try to find a better reason.

C. Americans do not like to think about being ill either, but this is not a reason to avoid drugstores. Try to find a better reason.

D. He does seem to be weight conscious with his remark about gaining 5 kilos (about 11 pounds) from his mother's cooking. In this case, it is not the talk about food that is making him angry. Use this hint and try again.

A. In this case, it is true she should not have said anything, but how long she may have known Rosa has nothing to do with it. Look for another answer.

B. She probably does prefer to look around the department store, but there is a more specific reason she does not want to go to the drugstore. Look at what she says and try again.

C. How many American boys would rather study than go to a movie? Besides, there are late afternoon matinees in Mexico, so he can go to a movie and still study in the evening as many Mexican students do. Find a better reason.

D. This might be partly true but if this were really the reason, he would have let her pay when she first suggested it. Try again.

A. Ruffy may be ugly. Some animals that North Americans find very lovable are not purebreds. However, this is not what is upsetting Maribel. Look for a different answer.

B. North Americans do seem to brag a lot and for this reason may be resented by people in other countries. But Tom really did not say that much about how well he plays. Try to find another reason that is more probable.

C. It is true Jesús is one expression that is used after someone sneezes, but in this conversation Mark has said that he is fine. Look for a different answer.

D. It is true that Latin Americans tend to have several first names (*nombres de pila*), but it is not customary for the boys to have their mother's name as one of them unless, perhaps, her name is María. Does this clue help you? Go back and try again.

A. While it is true that technology in many parts of Latin America is not as developed as in the U. S., this does not cause problems with such items as cameras, small appliances, TV sets and so on. There are many competent repairmen for such items and the North American will often be surprised at the low cost for such service. Read the conversation again to find out what Bob has not yet discovered about Latin Americans.

B. She might wish that she had ordered a tortilla now that it has arrived and she can see how good it looks; but she could still order one if she wished. There is a better explanation of why she is confused.

C. This might be true if it is an especially good dance, but it is not the specific reason that Eliseo and Dolores are staying.

D. This may be quite true since he shows familiarity with a wide range of poetry. But there is another reason why he is talking about poetry at this particular time. Try again.

A. Possibly, but probably not. Try again.

B. *Adiós* is not slang and it isn't the reason for the mistake. This expression is standard Spanish used consistently in certain situations. Can you find the reason?

C. Sr. Lombardi asked Grace for suggestions and if she thought of one that they liked, they would probably use it. Try again to find the best answer.

D. Maybe Marisol does not want to be bothered, but let's assume that she is really a very considerate person. After all, she offered to give Becky some of her paper. Try again.

A. Of course, one should make reservations during the tourist season in Spain because the hotels are extremely crowded. Even with reservations, you must take what the hotel has open. There is another answer that indicates the real misunderstanding.

B. Chavela says that she does not know the boy although the boy seems to know both Lynn and Chavela. Although it probably does bother Lynn that she does not know the boy, try to find a better reason for her annoyance.

C. While this may be true occasionally in the U. S., it is not the basis on which the day is celebrated in Latin America. Try again.

D. The old dog that they have is named *Nube* or Cloud and that is a tame name. There is another reason that they are rejecting her suggestions. Try again to find it.

A. It is true that all the names she is suggesting are American names in English, but that alone would not be a reason for them to reject her suggestions. There is something else that all her suggestions have in common. Does this hint help you to find the best answer?

B. Maybe he is. Maybe Debbie is rich since she is visiting in Puerto Rico. Try to find a better answer.

C. Who does? Try again.

D. Yes, he could do this, but as a typical Latin American, he probably will not. In the conversation, Diego says he will not pay the fine. In this case there is a more appropriate solution. Try again.

VOCABULARY

The Master Spanish-English Vocabulary presented here represents the vocabulary as it is used in the context of this book. The nouns are given in their singular form followed by their definite article only if they do not end in -o or -a. Adjectives are presented in their masculine singular form followed by -a. The verbs are given in their infinitive form followed by the reflexive pronoun –se if it is required, by the stem-change (ie), (ue), (i), by the orthographic change (c), (zc), by IR to indicate an irregular verb and by the preposition which follows the infinitive.

A

abrazar (c) to embrace, hug
abrir to open
abuela grandmother
acá here, over here
acabar to have just
  acabo de llegar I have just arrived
aceptar to accept
acomodadora usher
acordarse (ue) de to remember
acostumbrar to be accustomed
  acostumbrado, -a accustomed
activo, -a active
acuerdo agreement
  de acuerdo in agreement, agreed
adiós goodbye
¿adónde? (To) where
afición, la interest, hobby
afortunadamente fortunately
agradable pleasant
agradar to please
agradecer (zc) to be thankful for
agua, el water
ahí there
ahora now
  ahorita right now
álbum, el album
alegrarse de to be happy about
alegre cheerful, gay
algo something
alguien someone
algún some
almorzar (ue) (c) to eat lunch
almuerzo lunch
alto, -a tall
allá there

allí there
amable kind
amar to love
amarillo, -a yellow
americano, -a American
amigo friend
ángel, el angel
animado, -a lively
animal, el animal
anoche last night
ansia longing
antes before
anunciador, el announcer
año year
aprender to learn
aprobar (ue) to approve
aquí here
armario closet
arreglar to arrange, fix
arroz, el rice
arte, el art
artículo article
así so, thus, in this way, in that way, like this, like that
asiento seat
asociado, -a associated
asomar a to look out
aspirina aspirin
asunto matter, affair
aún even, still
aunque although
automovilístico, -a of automobiles
avenida avenue
avisar to inform, let (someone) know
¡Ay! Oh!
  ¡Ay de mí! Oh, my!
ayer yesterday
ayudar to help

B

bailar to dance
baile, el dance
bajar to go down, come down, get out
  bajar de peso to lose weight
banco bank
banda band
baño bathroom
barato, -a cheap
básicamente basically
bastante enough, fairly, rather
batido milk shake
bebida drink
bendito, -a blessed
biblioteca library
bien well, fine, good
  bien fría very cold
billete, el bill (money); ticket
biología biology
bisté beefsteak
blanco, -a white
bocacalle, la intersection
boda wedding
boleto ticket
bolsa purse
bonito, -a pretty
bosque, el woods
botones, el bellboy
brazo arm
brisa breeze
bueno, -a good, well
  buen good

C

caballería group of horseback riders
cabeza head
cada each, every
café, el coffee
cajero cashier
caliente hot, warm
calma calm, quiet
calor, el heat, warmth
  hace calor it is hot (weather)
  tiene calor she is hot
caluroso, -a warm
calle, la street
cama bed
cámara camera
camarero waiter
cambiar to change, exchange
camino road
camión, el bus (México)
campaña campaign
campeón, el champion
campo field
canción, la song
candidato candidate
canela cinnamon

cansado, -a tired
cantar to sing
¡caramba! My word!
carta letter
cartel, el showbill, program
casa house
  a casa home
  en casa at home
casarse (con) to marry, get married
casi almost
causa cause
cebolla onion
celebración, la celebration
celebrar to celebrate
cenar to eat supper
centavo cent, penny
centro center, downtown
cerca near
ceremonia ceremony
cerrar (ie) to close
  cerrado, -a closed
cien one hundred
cierto, -a certain
cinco five
cine, el movie
ciudad, la city
civil civil
¡claro! certainly!, of course!
clase, la class; kind, sort
clásico, -a classic
clavar to nail, fasten
clavel, el carnation
clima, el climate
clóset, el closet (Mex.)
club, el club
coca cola Coca Cola
cocinar to cook
cocinero cook
coche, el car
cochino pig; darn!, roadhog
cola line
colegio school (preparatory for the university)
comadre close friend
comedia play
comer to eat
cómico, -a comical, funny
comida meal; food
como as, like
  ¿cómo? how?
  ¡cómo no! of course!
compadre close friend
completo, -a complete
comprar to buy
  de compras shopping
comprender to understand
con with
concierto concert
conmigo with me
conocer (zc) to know, to become acquainted, to meet

contento, -a happy
contestar to answer
contigo with you
continuar to continue
control, el control
conversación, la conversation
copa wineglass
cortar to cut
cortesía courtesy
corto, -a short
correcto, -a correct
corredor, el corridor, hall
correo mail, post office
correr to run
corriente common, ordinary
cosa thing
costar (ue) to cost
creer IR to believe, think
criada maid
¿cuál? which?
cuando when
¿cuánto? how much?
cuarto one fourth, one quarter
cuarto room
cuatro four
cubano, -a Cuban
cueca a folk dance
cuenta check, bill
   darse cuenta de to realize
cuento story
cuerpo body
cuidado care
cumpleaños, el birthday
cumplir to fulfill, keep; comply with
   cumplir.... años to be ... years old
curioso, -a curious
curva curve

CH

chaqueta jacket
charlar to chat
chasco disappointment, trick
cheque, el check
chico boy
chistoso, -a funny, witty
chocarse (qu) to collide, hit
chocolate, el chocolate
chofer driver

D

dar IR to give
   dar un paseo to take a walk
   darse prisa to be in a hurry
deber, el duty
deber ought, should, ought to have, should
decir IR to say, tell
dejar to allow, let, leave

delgado, -a thin
delicioso, -a delicious
demócrata, el Democrat
dentro within
dependienta salesperson
deporte, el sport
derecha right
desayuno breakfast
descansar to rest
descanso rest period
descompuesto, -a broken, not working
descuento discount
desear to desire, want
después after, afterward
día, el day
diciembre December
dieta diet
diez ten
difícil difficult
dinero money
Dios God
dirección, la address
disco record
disfrutar de to enjoy, profit
divertirse (ie) to have a good time
   divertido amusing, entertaining
diversión, la amusement, entertainment
divino, -a divine
doce twelve
dólar, el dollar
doler (ue) to ache
dolor, el pain, ache
domingo Sunday
donde where
¿dónde? where?
¿adónde? (to) where
dos two
duda doubt
durante during
durar to last

E

echar to throw
   echar de menos to miss
   echar una fiesta to throw a party
edificio building
efectuar to carry out, accomplish
elección, la election
elegante elegant
embajada embassy
embarazada pregnant
embargo embargo
   sin embargo nevertheless
empezar (ie) (c) to begin
encantado, -a charmed
encontrar (ue) to find
   encontrarse con to meet
enfermo, -a sick, ill

enfrente in front of
enojarse to be angry
enojado, -a angry
ensalada salad
enseñar to teach, to show
entender (ie) to understand
entonces then, at that time
entrar to enter
entrada entrance
entre between, among
epidemia epidemic
error, el error
escribir to write
escuchar to listen
escuela school
ese that
   ése that one
espalda back
especial special
   especialmente especially
esperar to hope, wait, wait for
esposa wife
esquí acuático, el water skiing
estación, la station
estacionarse to park
estado state
   Estados Unidos United States
estar IR to be
este this
   éste this one
estrella star
estudiante, el, la student
estudiar to study
examen, el exam
excelente excellent
experto expert
explicar (qu) to explain
exposición, la exposition, show
exquisito, -a exquisite, lovely
extra extra

F

fácil easy
falta lack
   sin falta without fail
familia family
fantástico, -a fantastic, great
farmacia pharmacy, drug store
favor, el favor
   por favor please
feliz, felices happy
ferrocarril, el railroad
fiebre, la fever
fiesta party, holiday,
fila row
filosofía philosophy
fin, el end
   al fin finally
firmar to sign

flaquito, -a thin, skinny
flor, la flower
florero vase
formidable formidable, wonderful
foto, la photo, picture
freno brake
frío, -a cold
frito, -a fried
fuente, la fountain
fuerte strong
futbol, el football
futuro future

G

gana desire
   tener ganas de to feel like
ganadería cattle raising, livestock
ganado cattle
ganar to win, earn
garaje, el garage
gazpacho a Spanish soup
gente, la people
gobernador, el governor
gobierno government
golpe, el blow
   golpe de estado coup d'etat, sudden
      change of government
gozoso, -a joyful, cheerful, glad
gracias thank you
gracioso, -a amusing
grande big, large
gripe, la flu-like illness
grupo group
guapo, -a cute, good-looking
guardia, el guard, watchman
guía, el, la guide
gustar to like, be pleased
gusto pleasure

H

haber IR to have (used with perfect
   tenses)
habitación, la room
hablar to talk, speak
hacer IR to do, make
   hacer frío to be cold
hambre, la hunger
   tener hambre to be hungry
hambriento, -a hungry
hamburguesa hamburger
hasta until
   hasta la vista see you later
   hasta luego see you then
hermano brother
hermoso, -a beautiful
hielo ice
hígado liver
hijo son

hípico of horses
hispanoamericano, -a Spanish American
hola hello
hombre man
hombro shoulder
hora hour, time of day
horrible horrible
hospital, el hospital
hospitalidad, la hospitality
hotel, el hotel
hoy today
huelga strike
estar de huelga to be on strike
huevo egg

I

idea idea
igual equal
imaginarse to imagine
importar to be important
importante important
imposible impossible
incluir to include
increíble incredible, unbelievable
independiente independent
indígena native
indio Indian
infatigable untiring
infracción, la infraction
inmediatamente immediately
inscribirse to register
insistir to insist
insultar to insult
intercambio exchange
interesar to be interesting
interesante interesting
interesantísimo, -a very interesting
invitar to invite
invitación, la invitation
ir IR to go
izquierda left

J

jardín, el garden
jefe, el chief, boss, head
joven, el, la young person, youth
jueves Thursday
jugar (ue) to play (a game or sport)
jugo juice
julio July
junta council
juntos together

K

kilo kilogram (about 2.2 pounds)

L

ladrón, el thief, robber
lástima shame, pity
lavar to wash
leche, la milk
lechuga lettuce
leer IR to read
legumbre, la vegetable
lengua language
lenguaje, el language
lentamente slowly
letrero sign
levantarse to stand up, to sit up
liberación, la liberation
liberar to liberate, free
libertad, la liberty
libre free
librería bookstore
libro book
líder, el, la leader
limonada lemonade
lirio lily, iris
listo, -a ready
literatura literature
loco, -a crazy
lucir (zc) to shine, show off
luego then
luna moon
lunes Monday

LL

llamar to call
llamarse to be named
llanta tire
llegar to arrive
llevar to carry, take; to wear

M

macho male
madre mother
madrina godmother
madrina de bodas bridesmaid
magnífico, -a magnificent, great
malo, -a bad, ill
mamá mother
mandar to send
manejar to drive
manifestación, la demonstration
mañana tomorrow
maquillaje, el makeup
mar, el, la sea
maravilloso, -a marvellous
marca trademark, brand
marcharse to go, to leave
margarita daisy
marido husband
más more, most
matrimonio marriage

mayor older, oldest
medio half
medicina medicine
médico doctor
mediodía, el noon, midday
mejor better, best
mejoramiento improvement
mejorarse to improve, to get better
mencionar to mention
menos less, least
mercado market
mes, el month
   el mes que viene next month
mesa table
meterse en to meddle, to get mixed up in, to get into, to put oneself into
miedo fear
   tener miedo (de) to be afraid
mientras while
miércoles Wednesday
minuto minute
mío, -a mine
mirar to look, to look at
mismo, -a same
   ahora mismo right now
mitad, la half, middle
moda fashion, style
moderno, -a modern
modo manner, way
   de todos modos at any rate
molestarse to be bothered, disturbed
molestia bother, inconvenience
momento moment, minute
   momentito part of a moment, a second
mono monkey
monstruo monster
montaña mountain
   montaña rusa roller coaster
mordida bribe, bite
morir (ue) to die
   morirse to die, to be dying
movimiento movement
muchacho boy
mucho, -a much, very
   muchísimo, -a very much
mujer, la woman
multa fine
municipal municipal
muy very

N

nada nothing
nadie no one, nobody
naranja orange
necesario, -a necessary
necesitar to need
negocio business
negro, -a black
   negrita pretty black girl

nevar (ie) to snow
ni nor
nieve snow
ninguno, -a none, not any
niña girl
noche, la night
nombre, el name
norteamericano, -a North American, from the U. S.
notar to note, notice
noticia piece of news, notice
   noticias news
nube, la cloud
nuestro, -a our
nueve nine
nuevo, -a new
nunca never, not ever

Ñ

ñanduti, el fine, handmade Paraguayan lace

O

obrero worker, workman, laborer
observar to observe
ocupado, -a occupied, busy
ocurrir to occur, to happen
ochenta eighty
ocho eight
oficina office
oír IR to hear
ojalá I hope
ojo eye
olvidarse to forget
ómnibus, el bus
once eleven
opinar to have an opinion
opinión, la opinion
oportunidad, la opportunity
oriente, el East
otro, -a other, another

P

padre father
paella a food from Spain
pagar to pay
página page
país, el country
palacio palace
Palermo a district in Buenos Aires
pan, el bread
pantalones, los pants
papá Dad, father
papa potato
papel, el paper
para for, to, in order to

parecer (zc) to seem, appear, to seem like, to look like
pariente (-ta) el, la relative
parque, el park
parte, la part
participar to participate
particular particular
nada de particular nothing in particular
partido game, political party
pasado past
pasar to pass; come in, spend time; happen; take place
pasear to take a walk or a ride
paseo walk
pasillo hallway; aisle; corridor
pastel, el pastry
pastilla pill
pata paw
pedir (i) to ask, ask for; order a meal
peine, el comb
película film
peligroso, -a dangerous
pelo hair
pena pain; effort
pensar (ie) to think, to plan to, to intend to
pensión, la boarding house
pensión completa complete room; board and lodging
peor worse, worst
pepino cucumber
pequeño, –a small, little
perder (ie) to lose, to waste time
perfectamente perfectly
periódico newspaper
permitir to permit, allow
pero but
personalmente personally
perro dog
pesado, -a heavy, tiresome
pésame condolence
pesero a taxi with a fixed route
peso weight, unit of money
ganar peso to gain weight
piel, la skin
pirata pirate
piso floor, story of a building
plan, el plan
plátano banana
plato plate
playa beach
plaza plaza, town square
poco, -a little, few
poder (ue) to be able, can, may, be possible
no poder más not to be able to do more
poema, el poem
poesía poetry
política political

pollo chicken
poner IR to put, place, set
ponerse to put on, wear
popular popular
por by, through, because of; for, for the sake of, in behalf of, in return for; along; as
por acá over here, around here
por eso for that reason, thus
por favor please
por la tarde in the afternoon
¿por qué? why?
por supuesto of course
porque because
portarse to behave
posible possible
posibilidad, la possibility
posiblemente possibly
precaución, la precaution
precio price
preferir (ie) to prefer
preguntar to ask a question
premiar to give a prize, to award
preocuparse (de) to worry (about)
preparar to prepare
presentar to present, introduce
presidente (-ta), el, la president
presidencial of the president
prestar to lend, loan
pretendiente, el, la candidate, suitor
primero, -a first
primo, -a cousin
prisa haste, hurry
darse prisa to be in a hurry
probablemente probably
probarse (ue) to try on
problema, el problem
programa, el program
prohibido, -a prohibited, forbidden
prometer to promise
pronto soon
propio, -a own
propina tip
protección, la protection
puerta door
puertorriqueño, -a Puerto Rican
pues then, well
puesto place, booth, stand
puesto que since

Q

que which, that, who; than
¿qué? what?
quechua, el Indian language
quedarse to stay, remain; to fit
querer (ie) to want, wish
queso cheese
¿quién? who? whom?
quince fifteen
quizá perhaps

R

rápido, -a rapid, fast
raro, -a curious, strange
rato while
razón, la reason
  tener razón to be right
recepcionista receptionist
reconocer (zc) to recognize
refresco refreshment
regalo present, gift
regresar to return
  regreso return
reina queen
reír IR to laugh
reparar to repair
representante, el, la representative
representar to represent
republicano, -a Republican
reservación, la reservation
reservado, -a reserved
resfriado cold
restaurante, el restaurant
retiro retreat
reunión, la reunion, meeting
revista magazine
revolución, la revolution
rico, -a rich
ridículo, -a ridiculous
rioplatense from the area of the Río de la Plata in Argentina, Uruguay or Paraguay
romance, el romance
ropa clothes, clothing
rosa rose
roto, -a broken
Rotario Rotarian, from the Rotary Club
rudo, -a rude
ruso, -a Russian
  montaña rusa roller coaster

S

sábado Saturday
saber IR to know, know how
sabroso, -a delicious, savory
sacar (qu) to take out, to take a picture
sala living room
saleroso, -a charming, lively, witty
salir IR to leave, to go out
salto jump
saludar to greet
santo saint
sed, la thirst
  tener sed to be thirsty
seguir (i) to follow
segundo, -a second
seguro, -a sure, certain
seguridad, la security
seis six

semana week
sentir (ie) to feel, be sorry, regret
sentido, -a heartfelt, deeply felt
señor Mr., sir
señorita Miss, young woman
séptimo, -a seventh
ser IR to be
sereno watchman
serie, la series
serio, -a serious
servir (i) to serve
sesenta sixty
si if
sí yes
siempre always
siete seven
siguiente following, next
simpático, -a nice
sin without
  sin embargo nevertheless
sobre, el envelope
sobre over, above
sobrino nephew
social social
soda soda
sol, el sun
  hacer sol to be sunny
solamente only
sólo, -a only
sopa soup
sorprender to surprise
sorpresa surprise
subir to get on, to raise
sucio, -a dirty
suerte, la luck
  tener suerte to be lucky
suficiente sufficient, enough
sufrir to suffer
sugerencia suggestion
suponer IR to suppose
supuesto supposition
  por supuesto of course

T

tamaño size
también also, too
tampoco neither, not either
tan so, as
tanto, -a so, so much, as much
tarde, la afternoon; adj; late
tarjeta card
taxi, el taxi
teatro theater
techo roof, ceiling
tejado roof
teléfono telephone
telenovela pictorialized novel based on a TV program
televisión, la television

templado, -a temperate
temprano early
tener IR to have
  tener calor to be warm, hot
  tener ganas de to feel like
  tener hambre to be hungry
  tener razón to be right
  tener que to have to
  tener sed to be thirsty
tenis, el tennis
tercero, -a third
terminar to end
testigo witness
tiempo time, weather
tienda store
tío uncle
tiovivo merry-go-round
tipo type, a character
tocar (qu) to play music
  tocarse a uno to be one's turn
todavía still, yet
todo, -a all, every
tomar to take, drink
tomate tomato
tonto, -a foolish
tortilla a food
tostado toast
trabajo work
traer IR to bring
tráfico traffic
tragedia tragedy
traje, el suit
tránsito traffic
treinta thirty
tremendo, -a tremendous
tren, el train
tres three
triste sad
  tristísimo, -a very sad
turnar to take turns
turno turn

U

unido, -a united
  Estados Unidos United States
universidad, la university
unos, -as some
usar to use, to wear

V

vacación, la vacation
valenciano, -a Valencian
  paella valenciana a Spanish food
valer IR to be worth
varios, -as various, several
vaso glass
veinticinco twenty-five
velorio wake
vendedor, el salesperson
venir IR to come
  el jueves que viene next Thursday
ventaja advantage
ventanilla window, ticket window
ver IR to see
verdad, la true, truth; correct
verdadero, -a real, true
verde green
vestido dress
vez, la time
  a veces at times
  ¿cuántas veces? how many times?
  en vez de instead of
  muchas veces many times, often
  otra vez another time, again
  una vez one time, once
vida life
viejo, -a old
viernes Friday
vino wine
violinista violinist, fiddler
visitar to visit
visita visit, call
visitante, el, la visitor
vista scene, sight
vivir to live
volver to return
votar to vote

Y

y and
ya already

Z

zócalo main square, plaza
zona zone
zoológico zoo

NTC SPANISH CULTURAL AND LITERARY TEXTS AND MATERIAL

Contemporary Life and Culture
"En directo" desde España
Cartas de España
Voces de Puerto Rico
The Andean Region

Contemporary Culture—in English
Spain: Its People and Culture
Welcome to Spain
Life in a Spanish Town
Life in a Mexican Town
Spanish Sign Language
Looking at Spain Series

Cross-Cultural Awareness
Encuentros culturales
The Hispanic Way
The Spanish-Speaking World

Legends and History
Leyendas latinoamericanas
Leyendas de Puerto Rico
Leyendas de España
Leyendas mexicanas
Dos aventureros: De Soto y Coronado
Muchas facetas de México
Una mirada a España

Literary Adaptations
Don Quijote de la Mancha
El Cid
La Gitanilla
Tres novelas españolas
Dos novelas picarescas
Tres novelas latinoamericanas
Joyas de lectura
Cuentos de hoy
Lazarillo de Tormes
La Celestina
El Conde Lucanor
El burlador de Sevilla
Fuenteovejuna
Aventuras del ingenioso hidalgo
   Don Quijote de la Mancha

Civilization and Culture
Perspectivas culturales de España
Perspectivas culturales de Hispanoamérica

For further information or a current catalog, write:
National Textbook Company
a division of NTC *Publishing Group*
4255 West Touhy Avenue
Lincolnwood, Illinois 60646-1975 U.S.A.

0612